TRANZLATY

Language is for everyone

语言属于每个人

The Call of the Wild

野性的呼唤

Jack London

English / 普通话

Into the Primitive
进入原始

Buck did not read the newspapers.
巴克不看报纸。

Had he read the newspapers he would have known trouble was brewing.
如果他读过报纸，他就会知道麻烦即将来临。

There was trouble not alone for himself, but for every tidewater dog.
不仅他自己有麻烦，每一只潮水狗都遇到麻烦。

Every dog strong of muscle and with warm, long hair was going to be in trouble.
每只肌肉发达、毛发温暖且长的狗都会遇到麻烦。

From Puget Bay to San Diego no dog could escape what was coming.
从普吉特湾到圣地亚哥，没有一只狗能够逃脱即将发生的一切。

Men, groping in the Arctic darkness, had found a yellow metal.
人们在北极的黑暗中摸索，发现了一种黄色的金属。

Steamship and transportation companies were chasing the discovery.
轮船和运输公司都在追逐这一发现。

Thousands of men were rushing into the Northland.
数以千计的士兵涌入北国。

These men wanted dogs, and the dogs they wanted were heavy dogs.
这些人想要狗，而且他们想要的狗是重型狗。

Dogs with strong muscles by which to toil.
拥有强健肌肉、能吃苦耐劳的狗。

Dogs with furry coats to protect them from the frost.
狗有毛皮来抵御霜冻。

Buck lived at a big house in the sun-kissed Santa Clara Valley.

巴克住在阳光明媚的圣克拉拉谷的一所大房子里。

Judge Miller's place, his house was called.

这是米勒法官的住所，也就是他的房子。

His house stood back from the road, half hidden among the trees.

他的房子远离道路，半隐藏在树林中。

One could get glimpses of the wide veranda running around the house.

人们可以瞥见环绕房屋的宽阔阳台。

The house was approached by graveled driveways.

通往房屋的路是碎石车道。

The paths wound about through wide-spreading lawns.

小路蜿蜒穿过宽阔的草坪。

Overhead were the interlacing boughs of tall poplars.

头顶上是高大的白杨树交错的枝干。

At the rear of the house things were on even more spacious.

房子的后部空间更加宽敞。

There were great stables, where a dozen grooms were chatting

那里有大马厩，十几个马夫正在聊天

There were rows of vine-clad servants' cottages

有一排排爬满藤蔓的仆人小屋

And there was an endless and orderly array of outhouses

还有一排排整齐排列的户外厕所

Long grape arbors, green pastures, orchards, and berry patches.

长长的葡萄架、绿色的牧场、果园和浆果园。

Then there was the pumping plant for the artesian well.

然后还有自流井的抽水站。

And there was the big cement tank filled with water.

那里有一个装满水的大水泥罐。

Here Judge Miller's boys took their morning plunge.

米勒法官的儿子们在这里进行了晨间跳水。

And they cooled down there in the hot afternoon too.
在炎热的下午，它们也在那里降温。

And over this great domain, Buck was the one who ruled all of it.
在这片广阔的土地上，巴克是统治者。

Buck was born on this land and lived here all his four years.
巴克在这片土地上出生，并在这里度过了他一生的四年。

There were indeed other dogs, but they did not truly matter.
确实还有其他狗，但它们并不重要。

Other dogs were expected in a place as vast as this one.
在如此广阔的地方，预计还会有其他狗。

These dogs came and went, or lived inside the busy kennels.
这些狗来来去去，或者住在繁忙的狗舍里。

Some dogs lived hidden in the house, like Toots and Ysabel did.
有些狗像 Toots 和 Ysabel 一样，隐居在屋子里。

Toots was a Japanese pug, Ysabel a Mexican hairless dog.
图茨是一只日本哈巴狗，伊莎贝尔是一只墨西哥无毛犬。

These strange creatures rarely stepped outside the house.
这些奇怪的生物很少走出屋子。

They did not touch the ground, nor sniff the open air outside.
它们没有接触地面，也没有嗅到外面的空气。

There were also the fox terriers, at least twenty in number.
还有猎狐梗，数量至少有二十只。

These terriers barked fiercely at Toots and Ysabel indoors.
这些梗犬在室内对着 Toots 和 Ysabel 凶猛地吠叫。

Toots and Ysabel stayed behind windows, safe from harm.
图茨和伊莎贝尔躲在窗户后面，没有受到伤害。

They were guarded by housemaids with brooms and mops.
他们由拿着扫帚和拖把的女佣守护着。

But Buck was no house-dog, and he was no kennel-dog either.
但巴克不是家犬，也不是犬舍犬。

The entire property belonged to Buck as his rightful realm.
全部财产都属于巴克，是他的合法领地。

Buck swam in the tank or went hunting with the Judge's sons.
巴克在水箱里游泳或与法官的儿子们一起去打猎。

He walked with Mollie and Alice in the early or late hours.
他总是在清晨或深夜与莫莉和爱丽丝一起散步。

On cold nights he lay before the library fire with the Judge.
在寒冷的夜晚，他与法官一起躺在图书馆的火炉前。

Buck gave rides to the Judge's grandsons on his strong back.
巴克用它强壮的背背载着法官的孙子们。

He rolled in the grass with the boys, guarding them closely.
他和孩子们一起在草地上打滚，密切守护着他们。

They ventured to the fountain and even past the berry fields.
他们冒险前往喷泉，甚至穿过浆果田。

Among the fox terriers, Buck walked with royal pride always.
在猎狐梗中，巴克总是带着高贵的骄傲。

He ignored Toots and Ysabel, treating them like they were air.
他无视 Toots 和 Ysabel，把他们当空气一样对待。

Buck ruled over all living creatures on Judge Miller's land.
巴克统治着米勒法官土地上的所有生物。

He ruled over animals, insects, birds, and even humans.
他统治着动物、昆虫、鸟类，甚至人类。

Buck's father Elmo had been a huge and loyal St. Bernard.
巴克的父亲埃尔莫是一只体型巨大、忠诚的圣伯纳犬。

Elmo never left the Judge's side, and served him faithfully.
艾摩从未离开过法官的身边，并忠实地为他服务。

Buck seemed ready to follow his father's noble example.

巴克似乎准备效仿父亲的高尚榜样。

Buck was not quite as large, weighing one hundred and forty pounds.

巴克的体型没有那么大，体重只有一百四十磅。

His mother, Shep, had been a fine Scotch shepherd dog.

他的母亲谢普（Shep）是一只优秀的苏格兰牧羊犬。

But even at that weight, Buck walked with regal presence.

但即使体重如此之重，巴克走路时依然带着高贵的气质。

This came from good food and the respect he always received.

这源于他一直以来所受到的美食和尊重。

For four years, Buck had lived like a spoiled nobleman.

四年来，巴克过着像被宠坏的贵族一样的生活。

He was proud of himself, and even slightly egotistical.

他对自己很骄傲，甚至有点自负。

That kind of pride was common in remote country lords.

这种骄傲在边远的国主中很常见。

But Buck saved himself from becoming pampered house-dog.

但巴克避免了成为被宠坏的家犬。

He stayed lean and strong through hunting and exercise.

他通过狩猎和锻炼保持了精瘦和强壮。

He loved water deeply, like people who bathe in cold lakes.

他深爱水，就像在冷湖中沐浴的人一样。

This love for water kept Buck strong, and very healthy.

对水的热爱让巴克保持着强壮、健康的体魄。

This was the dog Buck had become in the fall of 1897.

这就是巴克在 1897 年秋天变成的那只狗。

When the Klondike strike pulled men to the frozen North.

当克朗代克矿脉将人们吸引到冰冻的北方时。

People rushed from all over the world into the cold land.

人们从世界各地涌入这片寒冷的土地。

Buck, however, did not read the papers, nor understand news.

然而，巴克不看报纸，也不懂新闻。

He did not know Manuel was a bad man to be around.

他不知道曼努埃尔是个坏人。

Manuel, who helped in the garden, had a deep problem.

在花园帮忙的曼努埃尔遇到了一个严重的问题。

Manuel was addicted to gambling in the Chinese lottery.

曼努埃尔沉迷于中国彩票赌博。

He also believed strongly in a fixed system for winning.

他也坚信固定的制胜体系。

That belief made his failure certain and unavoidable.

这种信念使他的失败成为必然和不可避免的结果。

Playing a system demands money, which Manuel lacked.

玩系统需要钱，而曼努埃尔缺乏钱。

His pay barely supported his wife and many children.

他的工资仅够养活他的妻子和几个孩子。

On the night Manuel betrayed Buck, things were normal.

曼努埃尔背叛巴克的那天晚上，一切都很正常。

The Judge was at a Raisin Growers' Association meeting.

法官当时正在参加葡萄干种植者协会的会议。

The Judge's sons were busy forming an athletic club then.

当时，法官的儿子们正忙着组建一个运动俱乐部。

No one saw Manuel and Buck leaving through the orchard.

没有人看到曼努埃尔和巴克穿过果园离开。

Buck thought this walk was just a simple nighttime stroll.

巴克以为这次散步只是一次简单的夜间散步。

They met only one man at the flag station, in College Park.

他们在学院公园的旗站只遇见了一个人。

That man spoke to Manuel, and they exchanged money.

那个男人和曼努埃尔交谈，然后他们交换了钱。

"Wrap up the goods before you deliver them," he suggested.

他建议道："发货前先把货物包好。"

The man's voice was rough and impatient as he spoke.

男人说话的声音很粗鲁，带着一丝不耐烦。

Manuel carefully tied a thick rope around Buck's neck.

曼努埃尔小心翼翼地将一根粗绳子绑在巴克的脖子上。

"Twist the rope, and you'll choke him plenty"

"拧动绳子，你就能把他勒死"

The stranger gave a grunt, showing he understood well.

陌生人咕哝了一声，表示他明白了。

Buck accepted the rope with calm and quiet dignity that day.

那天，巴克平静而庄重地接受了绳子。

It was an unusual act, but Buck trusted the men he knew.

这是一个不寻常的举动，但巴克信任他认识的人。

He believed their wisdom went far beyond his own thinking.

他相信他们的智慧远远超出了他自己的思维。

But then the rope was handed to the hands of the stranger.

但随后绳子就被交到了陌生人的手中。

Buck gave a low growl that warned with quiet menace.

巴克发出一声低沉的咆哮，带着无声的威胁和警告。

He was proud and commanding, and meant to show his displeasure.

他骄傲而威严，意在表达他的不满。

Buck believed his warning would be understood as an order.

巴克相信他的警告会被理解为命令。

To his shock, the rope tightened fast around his thick neck.

令他震惊的是，绳子紧紧地勒住了他粗壮的脖子。

His air was cut off and he began to fight in a sudden rage.

他的呼吸被切断，他突然愤怒地开始战斗。

He sprang at the man, who quickly met Buck in mid-air.

他向那人扑去，那人很快在半空中与巴克相遇。

The man grabbed Buck's throat and skillfully twisted him in the air.

那人抓住巴克的喉咙，熟练地将他扭到空中。

Buck was thrown down hard, landing flat on his back.

巴克被重重地摔倒，仰面朝天地摔在地上。

The rope now choked him cruelly while he kicked wildly.

当他疯狂地踢腿时，绳子残忍地勒住了他。

His tongue fell out, his chest heaved, but gained no breath.

他的舌头掉了下来，胸口起伏，但却没有呼吸。

He had never been treated with such violence in his life.

他一生中从未遭受过如此暴力的对待。

He had also never been filled with such deep fury before.

他也从来没有感到过如此强烈的愤怒。

But Buck's power faded, and his eyes turned glassy.

但巴克的力量逐渐减弱，他的眼神变得呆滞。

He passed out just as a train was flagged down nearby.

就在附近一列火车停下来时，他昏了过去。

Then the two men tossed him into the baggage car quickly.

随后两人迅速将他扔进行李车。

The next thing Buck felt was pain in his swollen tongue.

巴克接下来感觉到的是肿胀的舌头疼痛。

He was moving in a shaking cart, only dimly conscious.

他坐在摇晃的车里，意识模糊。

The sharp scream of a train whistle told Buck his location.

火车的尖锐汽笛声告诉了巴克他的位置。

He had often ridden with the Judge and knew the feeling.

他经常和法官一起骑马，所以了解这种感觉。

It was the unique jolt of traveling in a baggage car again.

这是再次乘坐行李车旅行时独特的震撼。

Buck opened his eyes, and his gaze burned with rage.

巴克睁开双眼，目光中燃烧着愤怒。

This was the anger of a proud king taken from his throne.

这是一位被从王位上赶下来的骄傲国王的愤怒。

A man reached to grab him, but Buck struck first instead.

一个人伸手去抓他，但巴克先动手了。

He sank his teeth into the man's hand and held tightly.

他咬住男人的手，紧紧地握住。

He did not let go until he blacked out a second time.

直到第二次昏过去，他才松手。

"Yep, has fits," the man muttered to the baggageman.
　"是的，发作了，" 那人对行李员低声说道。

The baggageman had heard the struggle and come near.
行李员听到了打斗声并走近了。

"I'm taking him to 'Frisco for the boss," the man explained.
　"我要带他去旧金山见老板，" 那人解释道。

"There's a fine dog-doctor there who says he can cure them."
　"那里有一位优秀的狗医生，他说他可以治好它们。
"

Later that night the man gave his own full account.
当晚晚些时候，该男子讲述了他的完整经历。

He spoke from a shed behind a saloon on the docks.
他在码头一家酒吧后面的棚子里发表了讲话。

"All I was given was fifty dollars," he complained to the saloon man.
　"我只得到了五十美元，" 他向酒吧服务员抱怨道。

"I wouldn't do it again, not even for a thousand in cold cash."
　"我不会再这么做了，哪怕是为了一千美元现金。"

His right hand was tightly wrapped in a bloody cloth.
他的右手被一块沾满鲜血的布紧紧包裹着。

His trouser leg was torn wide open from knee to foot.
他的裤腿从膝盖到脚被撕开了一道口子。

"How much did the other mug get paid?" asked the saloon man.
　"另一个家伙得到了多少钱？" 酒吧服务员问道。

"A hundred," the man replied, "he wouldn't take a cent less."
　"一百，" 那人回答，"少一分钱他也不会收。"

"That comes to a hundred and fifty," the saloon man said.
　"一共一百五十，" 酒吧老板说。

"And he's worth it all, or I'm no better than a blockhead."

"他值得我为他付出一切，否则我就和傻瓜没什么两样。"

The man opened the wrappings to examine his hand.
该男子打开包装纸检查他的手。

The hand was badly torn and crusted in dried blood.
这只手被严重撕裂，上面布满了干涸的血迹。

"If I don't get the hydrophobia..." he began to say.
"如果我没有得恐水症……"他开始说道。

"It'll be because you were born to hang," came a laugh.
"那是因为你生来就是要挂的，"一阵笑声传来。

"Come help me out before you get going," he was asked.
有人问道："走之前先来帮我一下。"

Buck was in a daze from the pain in his tongue and throat.
巴克因舌头和喉咙疼痛而陷入昏迷。

He was half-strangled, and could barely stand upright.
他被勒得半死，几乎站不起来。

Still, Buck tried to face the men who had hurt him so.
尽管如此，巴克还是试图面对那些伤害过他的人。

But they threw him down and choked him once again.
但他们又一次把他摔倒并勒住他的脖子。

Only then could they saw off his heavy brass collar.
只有这样，他们才能锯掉他沉重的黄铜项圈。

They removed the rope and shoved him into a crate.
他们解开绳子，把他塞进一个板条箱里。

The crate was small and shaped like a rough iron cage.
这个箱子很小，形状像一个粗糙的铁笼子。

Buck lay there all night, filled with wrath and wounded pride.
巴克整晚躺在那里，心中充满愤怒和受伤的自尊。

He could not begin to understand what was happening to him.
他无法理解自己身上到底发生了什么事。

Why were these strange men keeping him in this small crate?

这些陌生人为什么要把他关在这个小箱子里？

What did they want with him, and why this cruel captivity?

他们想要从他身上得到什么？为什么要对他进行如此残酷的囚禁？

He felt a dark pressure; a sense of disaster drawing closer.

他感到一股黑暗的压力；一种灾难正在逼近的感觉。

It was a vague fear, but it settled heavily on his spirit.

这是一种模糊的恐惧，但它却沉重地压在他的心头。

Several times he jumped up when the shed door rattled.

有好几次，当棚门嘎嘎作响时，他都跳了起来。

He expected the Judge or the boys to appear and rescue him.

他希望法官或男孩们出现并拯救他。

But only the saloon-keeper's fat face peeked inside each time.

但每次只有酒吧老板的胖脸向里面张望。

The man's face was lit by the dim glow of a tallow candle.

一支牛脂蜡烛昏暗的光芒照亮了男人的脸。

Each time, Buck's joyful bark changed to a low, angry growl.

每次，巴克欢快的吠叫都会变成低沉而愤怒的咆哮。

The saloon-keeper left him alone for the night in the crate

酒吧老板把他独自留在板条箱里过夜

But when he awoke in the morning more men were coming.

但当他早上醒来时，更多的人来了。

Four men came and gingerly picked up the crate without a word.

四个男人走了过来，一言不发地小心翼翼地抬起了板条箱。

Buck knew at once the situation he found himself in.

巴克立刻意识到自己所处的境地。

They were further tormentors that he had to fight and fear.

他们进一步折磨着他，他必须与之斗争，并惧怕他们。

These men looked wicked, ragged, and very badly groomed.

这些人看上去邪恶、衣衫褴褛，而且衣着很差。

Buck snarled and lunged at them fiercely through the bars.
巴克咆哮着，透过栅栏凶猛地向他们扑来。

They just laughed and jabbed at him with long wooden sticks.
他们只是大笑并用长木棍戳他。

Buck bit at the sticks, then realized that was what they liked.
巴克咬了咬树枝，然后意识到这就是它们喜欢的东西。

So he lay down quietly, sullen and burning with quiet rage.
于是他静静地躺下，闷闷不乐，心中却燃烧着愤怒。

They lifted the crate into a wagon and drove away with him.
他们把板条箱抬到一辆马车上，然后把他带走了。

The crate, with Buck locked inside, changed hands often.
巴克被锁在箱子里，箱子经常易手。

Express office clerks took charge and handled him briefly.
快递办公室的工作人员接手了此事，并对他进行了简单的处理。

Then another wagon carried Buck across the noisy town.
然后另一辆马车载着巴克穿过喧闹的小镇。

A truck took him with boxes and parcels onto a ferry boat.
一辆卡车将他连同箱子和包裹一起运上了渡船。

After crossing, the truck unloaded him at a rail depot.
过境后，卡车将他卸在了火车站。

At last, Buck was placed inside a waiting express car.
最后，巴克被安置在一辆等候的快车车厢里。

For two days and nights, trains pulled the express car away.
两天两夜，火车拉着特快车前行。

Buck neither ate nor drank during the whole painful journey.
在整个痛苦的旅途中，巴克既没吃也没喝。

When the express messengers tried to approach him, he growled.
当快递员试图接近他时，他发出咆哮声。

They responded by mocking him and teasing him cruelly.
他们以残酷的方式嘲笑和戏弄他。

Buck threw himself at the bars, foaming and shaking
巴克猛地扑向铁栏，口吐白沫，浑身发抖

they laughed loudly, and taunted him like schoolyard bullies.
他们大笑起来，像校园恶霸一样嘲笑他。

They barked like fake dogs and flapped their arms.
他们像假狗一样狂吠，并挥舞着手臂。

They even crowed like roosters just to upset him more.
它们甚至像公鸡一样啼叫，只是为了让他更加难过。

It was foolish behavior, and Buck knew it was ridiculous.
这是愚蠢的行为：巴克知道这很荒谬。

But that only deepened his sense of outrage and shame.
但这只会加深他的愤怒和羞耻感。

He was not bothered much by hunger during the trip.
旅途中他并没有太受饥饿的困扰。

But thirst brought sharp pain and unbearable suffering.
但口渴会带来剧烈的疼痛和难以忍受的痛苦。

His dry, inflamed throat and tongue burned with heat.
他的喉咙和舌头干燥发炎，灼热难耐。

This pain fed the fever rising within his proud body.
这种痛苦使他骄傲的身体里升起了高烧。

Buck was thankful for one single thing during this trial.
在这次审判中，巴克唯一感恩的就是一件事。

The rope had been removed from around his thick neck.
他粗壮脖子上的绳子已经解开了。

The rope had given those men an unfair and cruel advantage.
绳索给那些人带来了不公平且残酷的优势。

Now the rope was gone, and Buck swore it would never return.
现在绳子不见了，巴克发誓它永远不会回来。

He resolved no rope would ever go around his neck again.

他决心不再让绳子缠绕自己的脖子。

For two long days and nights, he suffered without food.
漫长的两天两夜，他没有吃东西，苦不堪言。

And in those hours, he built up an enormous rage inside.
在那几个小时里，他内心充满了愤怒。

His eyes turned bloodshot and wild from constant anger.
他的眼睛因持续的愤怒而变得布满血丝，充满狂野。

He was no longer Buck, but a demon with snapping jaws.
他不再是巴克，而是一个有着尖利下巴的恶魔。

Even the Judge would not have known this mad creature.
甚至连法官都不会认识这个疯狂的生物。

The express messengers sighed in relief when they reached Seattle
快递员们到达西雅图后松了一口气

Four men lifted the crate and brought it to a back yard.
四个男人抬起板条箱并将其运送到后院。

The yard was small, surrounded by high and solid walls.
院子不大，四周都是高大坚固的围墙。

A big man stepped out in a sagging red sweater shirt.
一个身材高大的男人穿着松垮的红色毛衣走了出来。

He signed the delivery book with a thick and bold hand.
他用粗壮的字体在交货簿上签名。

Buck sensed at once that this man was his next tormentor.
巴克立刻意识到这个人就是他的下一个折磨者。

He lunged violently at the bars, eyes red with fury.
他猛烈地向栅栏猛扑过去，眼睛里充满了愤怒。

The man just smiled darkly and went to fetch a hatchet.
那人只是阴沉地笑了笑，然后去拿一把斧头。

He also brought a club in his thick and strong right hand.
他还用粗壮有力的右手拿着一根球杆。

"You going to take him out now?" the driver asked, concerned.
司机担心的问道："你现在要带他出去吗？"

"Sure," said the man, jamming the hatchet into the crate as a lever.

"当然可以，" 男人说着，把斧头插进板条箱，当作杠杆。

The four men scattered instantly, jumping up onto the yard wall.

四个人立刻四散开来，跳上了院子的围墙。

From their safe spots above, they waited to watch the spectacle.

他们在上面的安全地点等待观看这一奇观。

Buck lunged at the splintered wood, biting and shaking fiercely.

巴克猛扑向碎木头，猛烈地咬着，颤抖着。

Each time the hatchet hit the cage), Buck was there to attack it.

每次斧头砍到笼子时，巴克都会攻击它。

He growled and snapped with wild rage, eager to be set free.

他狂怒地咆哮着、撕咬着，渴望得到释放。

The man outside was calm and steady, intent on his task.

外面的男人镇定而坚定，专心于自己的任务。

"Right then, you red-eyed devil," he said when the hole was large.

"好吧，你这个红眼魔鬼，" 当洞变大时，他说。

He dropped the hatchet and took the club in his right hand.

他扔掉斧头，用右手拿起棍棒。

Buck truly looked like a devil; eyes bloodshot and blazing.

巴克看起来真的像个魔鬼；眼睛里布满血丝，怒火中烧。

His coat bristled, foam frothed at his mouth, eyes glinting.

他的外套竖了起来，嘴里冒着泡沫，眼睛闪闪发光。

He bunched his muscles and sprang straight at the red sweater.

他绷紧肌肉，径直向红色毛衣扑去。

One hundred and forty pounds of fury flew at the calm man.

一百四十磅的愤怒向这个平静的男人袭来。

Just before his jaws clamped shut, a terrible blow struck him.
就在他咬紧牙关之前，他遭受了一次可怕的打击。

His teeth snapped together on nothing but air
他的牙齿在空气中咬合

a jolt of pain reverberated through his body
一阵剧痛传遍他的全身

He flipped midair and crashed down on his back and side.
他在半空中翻转，然后背部和侧面着地。

He had never before felt a club's blow and could not grasp it.
他以前从未感受过棍棒的打击，无法理解。

With a shrieking snarl, part bark, part scream, he leaped again.
他发出一声尖锐的咆哮，一半是吠叫，一半是尖叫，然后再次跳跃。

Another brutal strike hit him and hurled him to the ground.
又一次残酷的打击击中了他，并将他摔倒在地。

This time Buck understood—it was the man's heavy club.
这回巴克明白了——那是那人的沉重棍棒。

But rage blinded him, and he had no thought of retreat.
但愤怒蒙蔽了他的双眼，他没有退缩的念头。

Twelve times he launched himself, and twelve times he fell.
他跳伞十二次，坠落十二次。

The wooden club smashed him each time with ruthless, crushing force.
木棍每次都以无情、毁灭性的力量砸向他。

After one fierce blow, he staggered to his feet, dazed and slow.
猛烈的一击之后，他踉跄着站了起来，头晕目眩，行动迟缓。

Blood ran from his mouth, his nose, and even his ears.
他的嘴里、鼻子里、甚至耳朵里都流着血。

His once-beautiful coat was smeared with bloody foam.

他曾经美丽的外套上沾满了血迹斑斑的泡沫。

Then the man stepped up and struck a wicked blow to the nose.

然后那人走上前去，狠狠地打了他的鼻子一拳。

The agony was sharper than anything Buck had ever felt.

这种痛苦比巴克曾经感受过的任何痛苦都要剧烈。

With a roar more beast than dog, he leaped again to attack.

他发出一声比狗更像野兽的吼叫，再次跳跃起来发起攻击。

But the man caught his lower jaw and twisted it backward.

但那人抓住了他的下巴，并将其向后扭去。

Buck flipped head over heels, crashing down hard again.

巴克翻了个身，再次重重地摔倒在地。

One final time, Buck charged at him, now barely able to stand.

最后一次，巴克向他冲过来，现在他几乎站不起来。

The man struck with expert timing, delivering the final blow.

该名男子精准把握时机，给予了最后一击。

Buck collapsed in a heap, unconscious and unmoving.

巴克倒在地上，失去意识，一动不动。

"He's no slouch at dog-breaking, that's what I say," a man yelled.

"我说的是实话，他驯狗的技术真不错，" 一名男子喊道。

"Druther can break the will of a hound any day of the week."

"德鲁瑟可以在任何一天摧毁猎犬的意志。"

"And twice on a Sunday!" added the driver.

"而且是周日两次！" 司机补充道。

He climbed into the wagon and cracked the reins to leave.

他爬上马车，拉紧缰绳准备离开。

Buck slowly regained control of his consciousness

巴克慢慢恢复了意识

but his body was still too weak and broken to move.
但他的身体仍然虚弱无力，无法动弹。

He lay where he had fallen, watching the red-sweatered man.
他躺在倒下的地方，看着那个穿红毛衣的男人。

"He answers to the name of Buck," the man said, reading aloud.
"他的名字叫巴克，"那人大声读道。

He quoted from the note sent with Buck's crate and details.
他引用了巴克的板条箱随附的便条和详细信息。

"Well, Buck, my boy," the man continued with a friendly tone,
"好吧，巴克，我的孩子，"那人用友善的语气继续说道，

"we've had our little fight, and now it's over between us."
"我们刚刚吵了一架，现在一切都结束了。"

"You've learned your place, and I've learned mine," he added.
他补充道："你已经了解了自己的位置，我也了解了我的位置。"

"Be good, and all will go well, and life will be pleasant."
"心存善念，万事如意，生活就会幸福美满。"

"But be bad, and I'll beat the stuffing out of you, understand?"
"但如果你要是表现不好，我就把你打得落花流水，明白吗？"

As he spoke, he reached out and patted Buck's sore head.
他一边说着，一边伸手拍了拍巴克疼痛的头。

Buck's hair rose at the man's touch, but he didn't resist.
男人一碰巴克，他的汗毛就竖了起来，但他没有反抗。

The man brought him water, which Buck drank in great gulps.
那人给他拿来水，巴克大口大口地喝着。

Then came raw meat, which Buck devoured chunk by chunk.

接下来是生肉，巴克一块块地吃着。

He knew he was beaten, but he also knew he wasn't broken.

他知道自己被打败了，但他也知道自己没有被打败。

He had no chance against a man armed with a club.

面对一个手持棍棒的人，他毫无抵抗能力。

He had learned the truth, and he never forgot that lesson.

他已经了解了真相，并且永远不会忘记这个教训。

That weapon was the beginning of law in Buck's new world.

那件武器是巴克新世界中法律的开端。

It was the start of a harsh, primitive order he could not deny.

这是他无法否认的严酷、原始秩序的开始。

He accepted the truth; his wild instincts were now awake.

他接受了事实；他的狂野本能现在已经苏醒。

The world had grown harsher, but Buck faced it bravely.

世界变得越来越残酷，但巴克勇敢地面对。

He met life with new caution, cunning, and quiet strength.

他以新的谨慎、狡猾和沉着的力量面对生活。

More dogs arrived, tied in ropes or crates like Buck had been.

更多的狗来了，像巴克一样被绑在绳子或笼子里。

Some dogs came calmly, others raged and fought like wild beasts.

有些狗很平静地过来，有些则像野兽一样愤怒地打斗。

All of them were brought under the rule of the red-sweatered man.

他们全都被置于红毛衣男人的统治之下。

Each time, Buck watched and saw the same lesson unfold.

每次，巴克都会观察并看到同样的教训发生。

The man with the club was law; a master to be obeyed.

手持棍棒的人就是法律；是必须服从的主人。

He did not need to be liked, but he had to be obeyed.

他不需要被人喜欢，但他必须被人服从。

Buck never fawned or wagged like the weaker dogs did.

巴克从来不会像那些体弱的狗那样阿谀奉承或摇尾巴。

He saw dogs that were beaten and still licked the man's hand.

他看到被打的狗仍然舔着那个男人的手。

He saw one dog who would not obey or submit at all.

他看到一只根本不听话、不顺从的狗。

That dog fought until he was killed in the battle for control.

那只狗在争夺控制权的战斗中一直战斗到被杀死。

Strangers would sometimes come to see the red-sweatered man.

有时会有陌生人来看望这位穿红色毛衣的男人。

They spoke in strange tones, pleading, bargaining, and laughing.

他们用奇怪的语气说话、恳求、讨价还价、大笑。

When money was exchanged, they left with one or more dogs.

换完钱后，他们就带着一只或多只狗离开。

Buck wondered where these dogs went, for none ever returned.

巴克想知道这些狗去了哪里，因为它们都没有回来。

fear of the unknown filled Buck every time a strange man came

每当有陌生人来访时，巴克都会感到恐惧

he was glad each time another dog was taken, rather than himself.

每次被带走的是另一只狗而不是自己，他都很高兴。

But finally, Buck's turn came with the arrival of a strange man.

但最终，随着一个陌生男人的到来，巴克的转机到来了。

He was small, wiry, and spoke in broken English and curses.

他身材矮小，体格健壮，说着蹩脚的英语，还带着咒骂。

"Sacredam!" he yelled when he laid eyes on Buck's frame.
当他看到巴克的身影时，他大叫道："天哪！"

"That's one damn bully dog! Eh? How much?" he asked aloud.
"这真是条恶霸狗！嗯？多少钱？"他大声问道。

"Three hundred, and he's a present at that price,"
"三百，这价钱他算是一份礼物了。"

"Since it's government money, you shouldn't complain, Perrault."
"既然这是政府的钱，你就不应该抱怨，佩罗。"

Perrault grinned at the deal he had just made with the man.
佩罗对他刚刚与那人达成的交易笑了笑。

The price of dogs had soared due to the sudden demand.
由于需求突然增加，狗的价格也随之飙升。

Three hundred dollars wasn't unfair for such a fine beast.
对于这样一头好野兽来说，三百美元并不算不公平。

The Canadian Government would not lose anything in the deal
加拿大政府不会在交易中失去任何东西

Nor would their official dispatches be delayed in transit.
他们的官方公报也不会在运输途中延误。

Perrault knew dogs well, and could see Buck was something rare.
佩罗非常了解狗，他知道巴克是一种罕见的狗。

"One in ten ten-thousand," he thought, as he studied Buck's build.
当他观察巴克的体型时，他想："万分之一。"

Buck saw the money change hands, but showed no surprise.
巴克看到钱易手，但并不感到惊讶。

Soon he and Curly, a gentle Newfoundland, were led away.
很快，他和一只温顺的纽芬兰犬 卷毛 就被带走了。

They followed the little man from the red sweater's yard.

他们跟着小个子男人离开了穿红毛衣的院子。

That was the last Buck ever saw of the man with the wooden club.

那是巴克最后一次见到这个拿着木棍的男人。

From the Narwhal's deck he watched Seattle fade into the distance.

从独角鲸号的甲板上，他看着西雅图渐渐消失在远方。

It was also the last time he ever saw the warm Southland.

这也是他最后一次看到温暖的南国。

Perrault took them below deck, and left them with François.

佩罗把他们带到甲板下，交给弗朗索瓦。

François was a black-faced giant with rough, calloused hands.

弗朗索瓦是一个黑脸巨人，双手粗糙，长满老茧。

He was dark and swarthy; a half-breed French-Canadian.

他皮肤黝黑，是法裔加拿大混血儿。

To Buck, these men were of a kind he had never seen before.

对于巴克来说，这些人是他从未见过的。

He would come to know many such men in the days ahead.

在未来的日子里，他会认识许多这样的人。

He did not grow fond of them, but he came to respect them.

他并没有喜欢上他们，但却开始尊敬他们。

They were fair and wise, and not easily fooled by any dog.

他们公正而聪明，不会轻易被任何狗愚弄。

They judged dogs calmly, and punished only when deserved.

他们冷静地评判狗，只对应得的惩罚进行处罚。

In the Narwhal's lower deck, Buck and Curly met two dogs.

在独角鲸号的下层甲板上，巴克和卷毛遇到了两只狗。

One was a large white dog from far-off, icy Spitzbergen.

其中一只来自遥远冰冷的斯匹茨卑尔根岛的大白狗。

He'd once sailed with a whaler and joined a survey group.

他曾经跟随一艘捕鲸船航行并加入一个调查小组。

He was friendly in a sly, underhanded and crafty fashion.
他以一种狡猾、卑鄙和狡猾的方式表现出友好。

At their first meal, he stole a piece of meat from Buck's pan.
在他们第一次吃饭时，他从巴克的锅里偷了一块肉。

Buck jumped to punish him, but François's whip struck first.
巴克跳起来想要惩罚他，但弗朗索瓦的鞭子先打了过来。

The white thief yelped, and Buck reclaimed the stolen bone.
白人小偷大叫一声，巴克夺回了被偷的骨头。

That fairness impressed Buck, and François earned his respect.
这种公平给巴克留下了深刻的印象，弗朗索瓦也赢得了他的尊重。

The other dog gave no greeting, and wanted none in return.
另一只狗没有打招呼，也不希望得到任何回应。

He didn't steal food, nor sniff at the new arrivals with interest.
他没有偷食物，也没有对新来的人感兴趣地嗅嗅。

This dog was grim and quiet, gloomy and slow-moving.
这只狗冷酷而安静，阴郁而行动迟缓。

He warned Curly to stay away by simply glaring at her.
他只是怒视着 卷毛，警告她离她远点。

His message was clear; leave me alone or there'll be trouble.
他的意思很明确：别管我，否则会有麻烦。

He was called Dave, and he barely noticed his surroundings.
他叫戴夫，他几乎没有注意到周围的环境。

He slept often, ate quietly, and yawned now and again.
他经常睡觉，安静地吃饭，不时打哈欠。

The ship hummed constantly with the beating propeller below.
船底螺旋桨不停地轰鸣。

Days passed with little change, but the weather got colder.
日子一天天过去，天气没有什么变化，只是越来越冷
了。

Buck could feel it in his bones, and noticed the others did too.
巴克能够深刻地感受到这一点，并且注意到其他人也
同样如此。

Then one morning, the propeller stopped and all was still.
后来有一天早上，螺旋桨停了下来，一切都静止了。

An energy swept through the ship; something had changed.
一股能量席卷了整艘船；有些东西已经改变了。

François came down, clipped them on leashes, and brought them up.
弗朗索瓦走下来，用皮带牵着它们，然后把它们带了
上来。

Buck stepped out and found the ground soft, white, and cold.
巴克走了出去，发现地面又软又白，而且很冷。

He jumped back in alarm and snorted in total confusion.
他惊恐地跳了起来，困惑地哼了一声。

Strange white stuff was falling from the gray sky.
奇怪的白色物体从灰色的天空中落下。

He shook himself, but the white flakes kept landing on him.
他摇了摇身子，但白色的雪花仍然落在他身上。

He sniffed the white stuff carefully and licked at a few icy bits.
他仔细地嗅了嗅那白色的东西，并舔了几块冰。

The powder burned like fire, then vanished right off his tongue.
粉末像火一样燃烧，然后从他的舌头上消失了。

Buck tried again, puzzled by the odd vanishing coldness.
巴克又试了一次，他对奇怪消失的寒冷感到困惑。

The men around him laughed, and Buck felt embarrassed.
周围的人都笑了，巴克感到很尴尬。

He didn't know why, but he was ashamed of his reaction.

他不知道为什么，但他对自己的反应感到羞愧。

It was his first experience with snow, and it confused him.

这是他第一次见到雪，他感到很困惑。

The Law of Club and Fang
棍棒与尖牙法则

Buck's first day on the Dyea beach felt like a terrible nightmare.

巴克在戴亚海滩的第一天感觉就像一场可怕的噩梦。

Each hour brought new shocks and unexpected changes for Buck.

每一个小时都会给巴克带来新的震惊和意想不到的变化。

He had been pulled from civilization and thrown into wild chaos.

他被从文明社会中拉出来，陷入了混乱之中。

This was no sunny, lazy life with boredom and rest.

这不是一种阳光、懒散、无聊和休息的生活。

There was no peace, no rest, and no moment without danger.

没有和平，没有休息，也没有一刻不发生危险。

Confusion ruled everything, and danger was always close.

混乱笼罩着一切，危险近在咫尺。

Buck had to stay alert because these men and dogs were different.

巴克必须保持警惕，因为这些人和狗都不一样。

They were not from towns; they were wild and without mercy.

他们并非来自城镇；他们野蛮且无情。

These men and dogs only knew the law of club and fang.

这些人和狗只知道棍棒和尖牙的法则。

Buck had never seen dogs fight like these savage huskies.

巴克从未见过像这些凶猛的哈士奇一样打架的狗。

His first experience taught him a lesson he would never forget.

他的第一次经历给了他一个永生难忘的教训。

He was lucky it was not him, or he would have died too.

幸亏不是他，不然他也会死。

Curly was the one who suffered while Buck watched and learned.
当巴克观察并学习时，卷毛却遭受着痛苦。

They had made camp near a store built from logs.
他们在一座用原木搭建的商店附近扎营。

Curly tried to be friendly to a large, wolf-like husky.
卷毛（卷毛）
试图对一只体型巨大、像狼一样的哈士奇表现友好。

The husky was smaller than Curly, but looked wild and mean.
这只哈士奇比 卷毛 小，但看上去狂野而凶猛。

Without warning, he jumped and slashed her face open.
他毫无预兆地跳起来，划破了她的脸。

His teeth cut from her eye down to her jaw in one move.
他的牙齿一下子从她的眼睛咬到了下巴。

This was how wolves fought—hit fast and jump away.
这就是狼的战斗方式——快速攻击，然后跳开。

But there was more to learn than from that one attack.
但值得我们学习的东西远不止那次袭击。

Dozens of huskies rushed in and made a silent circle.
几十只哈士奇冲了进来，默默地围成一圈。

They watched closely and licked their lips with hunger.
他们仔细地观察着，饥渴地舔着嘴唇。

Buck didn't understand their silence or their eager eyes.
巴克不明白他们的沉默和热切的眼神。

Curly rushed to attack the husky a second time.
卷毛第二次冲向哈士奇发起攻击。

He used his chest to knock her over with a strong move.
他用胸部用力一击将她撞倒。

She fell on her side and could not get back up.
她倒在地上，无法再站起来。

That was what the others had been waiting for all along.
这正是其他人一直在等待的。

The huskies jumped on her, yelping and snarling in a frenzy.
哈士奇们跳到她身上，疯狂地尖叫和咆哮。

She screamed as they buried her under a pile of dogs.
当他们把她埋在一堆狗下面时，她尖叫起来。

The attack was so fast that Buck froze in place with shock.
攻击速度太快了，巴克吓得呆在原地。

He saw Spitz stick out his tongue in a way that looked like a laugh.
他看到斯皮茨伸出舌头，看起来像是在笑。

François grabbed an axe and ran straight into the group of dogs.
弗朗索瓦抓起一把斧头，径直冲进狗群。

Three other men used clubs to help beat the huskies away.
另外三名男子用棍棒帮忙把哈士奇赶走。

In just two minutes, the fight was over and the dogs were gone.
仅仅两分钟，战斗就结束了，狗也消失了。

Curly lay dead in the red, trampled snow, her body torn apart.
科莉死在了被踩踏的红色雪地里，她的身体被撕裂了。

A dark-skinned man stood over her, cursing the brutal scene.
一个皮肤黝黑的男人站在她面前，咒骂着这残酷的场面。

The memory stayed with Buck and haunted his dreams at night.
这段记忆一直留在巴克的心里，并让他夜里梦到这些事情。

That was the way here; no fairness, no second chance.
这就是这里的现状；没有公平，没有第二次机会。

Once a dog fell, the others would kill without mercy.
一旦有一只狗倒下，其他狗就会毫不留情地杀死它。

Buck decided then that he would never allow himself to fall.

巴克当时就决定，他决不允许自己跌倒。

Spitz stuck out his tongue again and laughed at the blood.
斯皮茨再次吐出舌头，对着鲜血大笑。

From that moment on, Buck hated Spitz with all his heart.
从那一刻起，巴克就打心底里恨起了斯皮茨。

Before Buck could recover from Curly's death, something new happened.
巴克还没来得及从卷毛的死中恢复过来，新的事情又发生了。

François came over and strapped something around Buck's body.
弗朗索瓦走了过来，用某样东西绑住了巴克的身体。

It was a harness like the ones used on horses at the ranch.
这是一种类似于牧场上马匹所用的马具。

As Buck had seen horses work, now he was made to work too.
巴克曾经见过马匹工作，现在他也必须工作。

He had to pull François on a sled into the forest nearby.
他必须用雪橇把弗朗索瓦拉进附近的森林。

Then he had to pull back a load of heavy firewood.
然后他又得拉回一担沉沉的柴火。

Buck was proud, so it hurt him to be treated like a work animal.
巴克很骄傲，所以被当作工作动物对待让他很伤心。

But he was wise and didn't try to fight the new situation.
但他很明智，并没有试图对抗新的情况。

He accepted his new life and gave his best in every task.
他接受了新的生活，并在每项任务中尽最大努力。

Everything about the work was strange and unfamiliar to him.
工作的一切对他来说都是陌生的、不熟悉的。

François was strict and demanded obedience without delay.
弗朗索瓦非常严格，要求下属毫不拖延地服从。

His whip made sure that every command was followed at once.

他的鞭子确保每条命令都立即得到执行。

Dave was the wheeler, the dog nearest the sled behind Buck.

戴夫是推车手，是巴克后面距离雪橇最近的狗。

Dave bit Buck on the back legs if he made a mistake.

如果巴克犯了错误，戴夫就会咬巴克的后腿。

Spitz was the lead dog, skilled and experienced in the role.

斯皮茨是领头犬，技术娴熟，经验丰富。

Spitz could not reach Buck easily, but still corrected him.

斯皮茨无法轻易接近巴克，但仍然纠正了他。

He growled harshly or pulled the sled in ways that taught Buck.

他严厉地咆哮着，或者用教导巴克的方式拉雪橇。

Under this training, Buck learned faster than any of them expected.

在这样的训练下，巴克的学习速度比他们任何人预想的都要快。

He worked hard and learned from both François and the other dogs.

他努力工作并向弗朗索瓦和其他狗学习。

By the time they returned, Buck already knew the key commands.

当他们回来时，巴克已经知道了关键的命令。

He learned to stop at the sound of "ho" from François.

他从弗朗索瓦那里学会了听到"ho"的声音就停下来。

He learned when he had to pull the sled and run.

他学会了何时拉着雪橇奔跑。

He learned to turn wide at bends in the trail without trouble.

他学会了在小路的弯道处轻松转弯。

He also learned to avoid Dave when the sled went downhill fast.

他还学会了当雪橇快速下坡时避开戴夫。

"They're very good dogs," François proudly told Perrault.

"它们是非常好的狗，" 弗朗索瓦自豪地告诉佩罗。

"That Buck pulls like hell—I teach him quick as anything."

"那只巴克拉东西非常厉害——
我教他速度非常快。"

Later that day, Perrault came back with two more husky
dogs.

当天晚些时候，佩罗又带着两只哈士奇犬回来了。

Their names were Billee and Joe, and they were brothers.

他们的名字是比利（Billee）和乔
（Joe），他们是兄弟。

They came from the same mother, but were not alike at all.

他们虽然出自同一个母亲，但却完全不同。

Billee was sweet-natured and too friendly with everyone.

Billee 性格温和，对每个人都很友好。

Joe was the opposite—quiet, angry, and always snarling.

乔则相反——安静、易怒，而且总是咆哮。

Buck greeted them in a friendly way and was calm with
both.

巴克以友好的方式向他们打招呼，并且对两人都很平
静。

Dave paid no attention to them and stayed silent as usual.

戴夫没有理会他们，像往常一样保持沉默。

Spitz attacked first Billee, then Joe, to show his dominance.

斯皮茨首先攻击比利，然后是乔，以显示他的统治地
位。

Billee wagged his tail and tried to be friendly to Spitz.

比利摇着尾巴，试图对斯皮茨表现得友好。

When that didn't work, he tried to run away instead.

当此举无效时，他更试图逃跑。

He cried sadly when Spitz bit him hard on the side.

当斯皮茨用力咬他的侧面时，他伤心地哭了。

But Joe was very different and refused to be bullied.

但乔却截然不同，他拒绝被欺负。

Every time Spitz came near, Joe spun to face him fast.
每次斯皮茨靠近，乔就会快速转身面对他。

His fur bristled, his lips curled, and his teeth snapped wildly.
他的毛发竖了起来，嘴唇卷曲，牙齿疯狂地咬着。

Joe's eyes gleamed with fear and rage, daring Spitz to strike.
乔的眼里闪烁着恐惧和愤怒，挑衅斯皮茨并发起攻击。

Spitz gave up the fight and turned away, humiliated and angry.
斯皮茨放弃了反抗，转身离开，感到羞辱和愤怒。

He took out his frustration on poor Billee and chased him away.
他把自己的沮丧发泄在可怜的比利身上，并把他赶走了。

That evening, Perrault added one more dog to the team.
那天晚上，佩罗的队伍里又增加了一只狗。

This dog was old, lean, and covered in battle scars.
这只狗又老又瘦，浑身都是战争留下的伤疤。

One of his eyes was missing, but the other flashed with power.
他的一只眼睛不见了，但另一只眼睛却闪烁着力量。

The new dog's name was Solleks, which meant the Angry One.
这只新狗的名字叫 Solleks，意思是"愤怒的人"。

Like Dave, Solleks asked nothing from others, and gave nothing back.
和戴夫一样，索莱克斯不向别人索取任何东西，也不给予任何回报。

When Solleks walked slowly into camp, even Spitz stayed away.
当索莱克斯慢慢走进营地时，就连斯皮茨也躲开了。

He had a strange habit that Buck was unlucky to discover.
他有一个奇怪的习惯，巴克很不幸地发现了这一点。

Solleks hated being approached on the side where he was blind.

索莱克斯讨厌别人从他看不见的地方接近他。

Buck did not know this and made that mistake by accident.

巴克不知道这一点，所以无意中犯了这个错误。

Solleks spun around and slashed Buck's shoulder deep and fast.

索莱克斯旋转身子，迅速而深地砍向巴克的肩膀。

From that moment on, Buck never came near Solleks' blind side.

从那一刻起，巴克再也没有靠近索莱克斯的盲区。

They never had trouble again for the rest of their time together.

在他们在一起的剩余时间里，他们再也没有遇到过麻烦。

Solleks wanted only to be left alone, like quiet Dave.

索莱克斯只想独处，就像安静的戴夫一样。

But Buck would later learn they each had another secret goal.

但巴克后来得知，他们各自都有另一个秘密目标。

That night Buck faced a new and troubling challenge—how to sleep.

那天晚上，巴克面临着一个新的、令人困扰的挑战——如何入睡。

The tent glowed warmly with candlelight in the snowy field.

雪原上的帐篷在烛光的照耀下显得温暖。

Buck walked inside, thinking he could rest there like before.

巴克走了进去，心想他可以像以前一样在那里休息。

But Perrault and François yelled at him and threw pans.

但佩罗和弗朗索瓦对他大喊大叫，并扔平底锅。

Shocked and confused, Buck ran out into the freezing cold.

巴克感到震惊和困惑，便跑进了严寒之中。

A bitter wind stung his wounded shoulder and froze his paws.

凛冽的寒风刺痛了他受伤的肩膀，冻僵了他的爪子。

He lay down in the snow and tried to sleep out in the open.
他躺在雪地里，试图在户外睡觉。

But the cold soon forced him to get back up, shaking badly.
但寒冷很快迫使他站起来，浑身颤抖。

He wandered through the camp, trying to find a warmer spot.
他在营地里徘徊，试图找到一个更温暖的地方。

But every corner was just as cold as the one before.
但每个角落都和之前一样冷。

Sometimes savage dogs jumped at him from the darkness.
有时，凶猛的狗会从黑暗中向他扑来。

Buck bristled his fur, bared his teeth, and snarled with warning.
巴克竖起身上的毛，露出牙齿，发出警告性的咆哮声。

He was learning fast, and the other dogs backed off quickly.
他学得很快，其他狗也很快就退缩了。

Still, he had no place to sleep, and no idea what to do.
但他没有地方睡觉，也不知道该怎么办。

At last, a thought came to him—check on his team-mates.
最后，他想到了一个主意——去看看他的队友。

He returned to their area and was surprised to find them gone.
他回到他们所在的地方，惊讶地发现他们已经不见了。

Again he searched the camp, but still could not find them.
他再次搜寻营地，但仍然没有找到他们。

He knew they could not be in the tent, or he would be too.
他知道他们不能在帐篷里，否则他也会进去。

So where had all the dogs gone in this frozen camp?
那么，这个冰冻营地里的狗都到哪里去了呢？

Buck, cold and miserable, slowly circled around the tent.
巴克感到寒冷和痛苦，他慢慢地绕着帐篷转了一圈。

Suddenly, his front legs sank into soft snow and startled him.

突然，他的前腿陷入了柔软的雪中，把他吓了一跳。

Something wriggled under his feet, and he jumped back in fear.

有什么东西在他脚下蠕动，他吓得往后跳了一步。

He growled and snarled, not knowing what lay beneath the snow.

他咆哮着，不知道雪下有什么。

Then he heard a friendly little bark that eased his fear.

然后他听到一声友好的小吠声，减轻了他的恐惧。

He sniffed the air and came closer to see what was hidden.

他嗅了嗅空气，走近去看隐藏着什么。

Under the snow, curled into a warm ball, was little Billee.

在雪下，小比莉蜷缩成一个温暖的球。

Billee wagged his tail and licked Buck's face to greet him.

比利摇着尾巴，舔着巴克的脸来向他打招呼。

Buck saw how Billee had made a sleeping place in the snow.

巴克看到比莉在雪地里挖了一个睡觉的地方。

He had dug down and used his own heat to stay warm.

他挖了个洞，用自己的热量来取暖。

Buck had learned another lesson—this was how the dogs slept.

巴克又学到了另一个教训——这就是狗的睡觉方式。

He picked a spot and started digging his own hole in the snow.

他选了一个地方并开始在雪地里挖洞。

At first, he moved around too much and wasted energy.

一开始，他走动太多，浪费了精力。

But soon his body warmed the space, and he felt safe.

但很快他的身体就温暖了起来，他感到安全了。

He curled up tightly, and before long he was fast asleep.

他紧紧地蜷缩着身子，不久就睡着了。

The day had been long and hard, and Buck was exhausted.

这一天漫长而艰难，巴克已经筋疲力尽了。

He slept deeply and comfortably, though his dreams were wild.
尽管他的梦很狂野，但他睡得很沉很舒服。
He growled and barked in his sleep, twisting as he dreamed.
他在睡梦中咆哮、吠叫，在梦中扭动身体。

Buck didn't wake up until the camp was already coming to life.
直到营地开始热闹起来，巴克才醒来。
At first, he didn't know where he was or what had happened.
起初，他不知道自己在哪里，也不知道发生了什么事。
Snow had fallen overnight and completely buried his body.
一夜之间，大雪降临，将他的尸体彻底掩埋。
The snow pressed in around him, tight on all sides.
雪紧紧地包围着他。
Suddenly a wave of fear rushed through Buck's entire body.
突然间，一股恐惧感涌遍巴克全身。
It was the fear of being trapped, a fear from deep instincts.
这是一种被困住的恐惧，一种发自内心的本能的恐惧。
Though he had never seen a trap, the fear lived inside him.
尽管他从未见过陷阱，但恐惧却一直萦绕在他的心头。
He was a tame dog, but now his old wild instincts were waking.
他曾经是一只温顺的狗，但是现在他昔日的野性本能正在苏醒。
Buck's muscles tensed, and his fur stood up all over his back.
巴克的肌肉绷紧了，背上的毛都竖了起来。
He snarled fiercely and sprang straight up through the snow.
他凶狠地咆哮一声，直接从雪地里跳了起来。

Snow flew in every direction as he burst into the daylight.
当他冲进阳光下时，雪花四处飞扬。

Even before landing, Buck saw the camp spread out before him.
甚至在着陆之前，巴克就看到营地在他面前展开。

He remembered everything from the day before, all at once.
他一下子想起了前一天发生的一切。

He remembered strolling with Manuel and ending up in this place.
他记得和曼努埃尔一起散步，最后来到这个地方。

He remembered digging the hole and falling asleep in the cold.
他记得自己挖了个洞，然后在寒冷中睡着了。

Now he was awake, and the wild world around him was clear.
现在他醒了，周围的荒野世界变得清晰起来。

A shout from François hailed Buck's sudden appearance.
弗朗索瓦大声喊叫，欢迎巴克的突然出现。

"What did I say?" the dog-driver cried loudly to Perrault.
"我说了什么？"狗司机大声向佩罗喊道。

"That Buck for sure learns quick as anything," François added.
"巴克学东西的速度确实很快，"弗朗索瓦补充道。

Perrault nodded gravely, clearly pleased with the result.
佩罗严肃地点了点头，显然对结果很满意。

As a courier for the Canadian Government, he carried dispatches.
作为加拿大政府的一名信使，他负责递送急件。

He was eager to find the best dogs for his important mission.
他渴望找到最适合他重要使命的狗。

He felt especially pleased now that Buck was part of the team.
现在巴克已经成为团队的一员，他感到特别高兴。

Three more huskies were added to the team within an hour.
不到一个小时，队伍里又增加了三只哈士奇。

That brought the total number of dogs on the team to nine.
这样，队伍里的狗总数就达到了九只。

Within fifteen minutes all the dogs were in their harnesses.
十五分钟之内，所有的狗都套上了挽具。

The sled team was swinging up the trail toward Dyea Cañon.
雪橇队正沿着小路向戴亚峡谷（Dyea Cañon）驶去。

Buck felt glad to be leaving, even if the work ahead was hard.
尽管前面的工作很艰辛，但巴克还是很高兴能够离开。

He found he did not particularly despise the labor or the cold.
他发现自己并不特别厌恶劳动或寒冷。

He was surprised by the eagerness that filled the whole team.
他对整个团队所展现出的热情感到惊讶。

Even more surprising was the change that had come over Dave and Solleks.
更令人惊讶的是戴夫和索莱克斯身上发生的变化。

These two dogs were entirely different when they were harnessed.
这两只狗戴上挽具后的样子截然不同。

Their passiveness and lack of concern had completely disappeared.
他们的被动和漠不关心已经完全消失了。

They were alert and active, and eager to do their work well.
他们精神矍铄、积极主动，渴望做好自己的工作。

They grew fiercely irritated at anything that caused delay or confusion.
任何导致延误或混乱的事情都会让他们非常恼火。

The hard work on the reins was the center of their entire being.
辛苦驾驭缰绳是他们全部精力的中心。

Sled pulling seemed to be the only thing they truly enjoyed.

拉雪橇似乎是他们唯一真正喜欢的事情。

Dave was at the back of the group, closest to the sled itself.

戴夫位于队伍的最后面，距离雪橇最近。

Buck was placed in front of Dave, and Solleks pulled ahead of Buck.

巴克被安排在戴夫前面，而索莱克斯则领先于巴克。

The rest of the dogs were strung out ahead in a single file.

其余的狗则排成一列纵队走在前面。

The lead position at the front was filled by Spitz.

最前面的领先位置由施皮茨占据。

Buck had been placed between Dave and Solleks for instruction.

巴克被安排在戴夫和索莱克斯之间接受指导。

He was a quick learner, and they were firm and capable teachers.

他学东西很快，他们是坚定而能干的老师。

They never allowed Buck to remain in error for long.

他们从不允许巴克长时间犯错。

They taught their lessons with sharp teeth when needed.

必要时，他们会用尖锐的言辞传授知识。

Dave was fair and showed a quiet, serious kind of wisdom.

戴夫很公平，并且表现出一种安静、严肃的智慧。

He never bit Buck without a good reason to do so.

他从来不会无缘无故地咬巴克。

But he never failed to bite when Buck needed correction.

但当巴克需要纠正时，他总是会咬巴克。

François's whip was always ready and backed up their authority.

弗朗索瓦的鞭子随时准备着，以支持他们的权威。

Buck soon found it was better to obey than to fight back.

巴克很快发现服从比反击更好。

Once, during a short rest, Buck got tangled in the reins.

有一次，在短暂的休息期间，巴克被缰绳缠住了。

He delayed the start and confused the team's movement.

他推迟了比赛的开始，扰乱了球队的行动。

Dave and Solleks flew at him and gave him a rough beating.
戴夫和索莱克斯向他扑去，狠狠地揍了他一顿。

The tangle only got worse, but Buck learned his lesson well.
纠缠变得越来越严重，但巴克很好地吸取了教训。

From then on, he kept the reins taut, and worked carefully.
从此以后，他严守纪律，认真工作。

Before the day ended, Buck had mastered much of his task.
在这一天结束之前，巴克已经完成了大部分任务。

His teammates almost stopped correcting or biting him.
他的队友几乎不再纠正他或咬他。

François's whip cracked through the air less and less often.
弗朗索瓦的鞭子在空中划过的声音越来越小。

Perrault even lifted Buck's feet and carefully examined each paw.
佩罗甚至抬起巴克的脚，仔细检查每只爪子。

It had been a hard day's run, long and exhausting for them all.
对于他们所有人来说，这是艰苦的一天，漫长而疲惫。

They travelled up the Cañon, through Sheep Camp, and past the Scales.
他们沿着峡谷向上行进，穿过羊营（Sheep Camp），经过斯凯尔斯（Scales）。

They crossed the timber line, then glaciers and snowdrifts many feet deep.
他们越过林木线，然后穿过数英尺深的冰川和雪堆。

They climbed the great cold and forbidding Chilkoot Divide.
他们翻越了极其寒冷和险峻的奇尔库特分水岭。

That high ridge stood between salt water and the frozen interior.
那道高高的山脊矗立在咸水和冰冻的内陆之间。

The mountains guarded the sad and lonely North with ice and steep climbs.

群山以冰雪和陡峭的山坡守护着悲伤而孤独的北方。

They made good time down a long chain of lakes below the divide.

他们顺利地穿过了分水岭下方的一长串湖泊。

Those lakes filled the ancient craters of extinct volcanoes.

这些湖泊填满了古老的死火山口。

Late that night, they reached a large camp at Lake Bennett.

那天深夜，他们到达了班尼特湖的一个大营地。

Thousands of gold seekers were there, building boats for spring.

数以千计的淘金者在那里建造船只，以备春天之用。

The ice was going break up soon, and they had to be ready.

冰很快就要破裂了，他们必须做好准备。

Buck dug his hole in the snow and fell into a deep sleep.

巴克在雪地里挖了一个洞，然后沉沉地睡去。

He slept like a working man, exhausted from the harsh day of toil.

他像一个工作的人一样睡着了，因为辛苦劳作了一天而精疲力尽。

But too early in the darkness, he was dragged from sleep.

但在天黑得太早的时候，他就被从睡梦中惊醒了。

He was harnessed with his mates again and attached to the sled.

他再次与伙伴们套上挽具并系在雪橇上。

That day they made forty miles, because the snow was well trodden.

那天他们走了四十英里，因为雪被踩得很深。

The next day, and for many days after, the snow was soft.

第二天以及之后的许多天，雪都很软。

They had to make the path themselves, working harder and moving slower.

他们必须自己开辟道路，工作更加努力，但进展却更慢。

Usually, Perrault walked ahead of the team with webbed snowshoes.

通常，佩罗会穿着带蹼的雪鞋走在队伍前面。

His steps packed the snow, making it easier for the sled to move.

他的脚步踩实了雪地，使雪橇更容易移动。

François, who steered from the gee-pole, sometimes took over.

弗朗索瓦有时会利用船舵杆掌舵。

But it was rare that François took the lead

但弗朗索瓦很少带头

because Perrault was in a rush to deliver the letters and parcels.

因为佩罗急着递送信件和包裹。

Perrault was proud of his knowledge of snow, and especially ice.

佩罗对自己对雪，特别是冰的了解感到自豪。

That knowledge was essential, because fall ice was dangerously thin.

这些知识至关重要，因为秋季冰层非常薄，非常危险。

Where water flowed fast beneath the surface, there was no ice at all.

在水面下快速流动的地方，根本没有冰。

Day after day, the same routine repeated without end.

日复一日，同样的例行公事无休止地重复着。

Buck toiled endlessly in the reins from dawn until night.

巴克从黎明到夜晚不停地操练缰绳。

They left camp in the dark, long before the sun had risen.

他们在天黑时离开了营地，那时太阳还未升起。

By the time daylight came, many miles were already behind them.

天亮的时候，他们已经走了好几英里了。

They pitched camp after dark, eating fish and burrowing into snow.

天黑后他们扎营，吃鱼，在雪地里挖洞。

Buck was always hungry and never truly satisfied with his ration.

巴克总是感到饥饿，并且从来都没有真正对他的食物感到满足。

He received a pound and a half of dried salmon each day.

他每天能收到一磅半的干鲑鱼。

But the food seemed to vanish inside him, leaving hunger behind.

但食物似乎在他体内消失了，只剩下饥饿感。

He suffered from constant pangs of hunger, and dreamed of more food.

他经常感到饥饿，梦想着能有更多的食物。

The other dogs got only one pound of food, but they stayed strong.

其他狗只得到了一磅食物，但它们仍然坚强。

They were smaller, and had been born into the northern life.

它们体型较小，出生在北方。

He swiftly lost the fastidiousness which had marked his old life.

他很快就不再像以前那样一丝不苟。

He had been a dainty eater, but now that was no longer possible.

他以前是个很讲究饮食的人，但是现在不再可能了。

His mates finished first and robbed him of his unfinished ration.

他的同伴们先吃完了，并抢走了他未吃完的口粮。

Once they began there was no way to defend his food from them.

一旦它们开始攻击他，他就没有任何办法可以保护自己的食物了。

While he fought off two or three dogs, the others stole the rest.

当他击退两三只狗时，其余的狗就被其他狗偷走了。

To fix this, he began eating as fast as the others ate.

为了解决这个问题，他开始和其他人一样快地吃饭。

Hunger pushed him so hard that he even took food not his own.
饥饿使他难以忍受，他甚至吃掉不是自己的食物。
He watched the others and learned quickly from their actions.
他观察其他人并很快从他们的行为中学习。
He saw Pike, a new dog, steal a slice of bacon from Perrault.
他看到一只新狗派克从佩罗那里偷了一片培根。
Pike had waited until Perrault's back was turned to steal the bacon.
派克一直等到佩罗转过身去偷培根。
The next day, Buck copied Pike and stole the whole chunk.
第二天，巴克模仿派克，偷走了整块石头。
A great uproar followed, but Buck was not suspected.
随后发生了一场大骚动，但巴克并没有受到怀疑。
Dub, a clumsy dog who always got caught, was punished instead.
笨手笨脚的狗杜布总是被抓住，因此受到了惩罚。
That first theft marked Buck as a dog fit to survive the North.
第一次偷窃事件标志着巴克是一只适合在北方生存的狗。
He showed he could adapt to new conditions and learn quickly.
他表现出他能够适应新环境并快速学习。
Without such adaptability, he would have died swiftly and badly.
如果没有这样的适应能力，他就会死得又快又惨。
It also marked the breakdown of his moral nature and past values.
这也标志着他的道德本质和过去价值观的崩溃。
In the Southland, he had lived under the law of love and kindness.
在南国，他生活在充满爱与仁慈的法律之下。

There it made sense to respect property and other dogs'
feelings.

在那里，尊重财产和其他狗的感受是有道理的。

But the Northland followed the law of club and the law of
fang.

但北国遵循的是棍棒法则和尖牙法则。

Whoever respected old values here was foolish and would
fail.

任何尊重这里旧价值观的人都是愚蠢的，都会失败。

Buck did not reason all this out in his mind.

巴克心里并没有想清楚这一切。

He was fit, and so he adjusted without needing to think.

他身体很健康，所以不用思考就能调整。

All his life, he had never run away from a fight.

他一生中从未逃避过战斗。

But the wooden club of the man in the red sweater changed
that rule.

但穿红毛衣的男人的木棍改变了这个规则。

Now he followed a deeper, older code written into his being.

现在，他遵循着刻在他心中的更深层、更古老的准则
。

He did not steal out of pleasure, but from the pain of
hunger.

他偷窃并非出于享乐，而是因为饥饿的痛苦。

He never robbed openly, but stole with cunning and care.

他从不公开抢劫，而是狡猾而谨慎地偷窃。

He acted out of respect for the wooden club and fear of the
fang.

他的行为是出于对木棍的尊重和对毒牙的恐惧。

In short, he did what was easier and safer than not doing it.

简而言之，他做的比不做的更容易、更安全。

His development—or perhaps his return to old instincts—
was fast.

他的成长——或者说他恢复旧有本能——非常快。

His muscles hardened until they felt as strong as iron.

他的肌肉变得越来越结实，直到感觉像铁一样坚硬。

He no longer cared about pain, unless it was serious.

他不再关心疼痛，除非疼痛很严重。

He became efficient inside and out, wasting nothing at all.

他从内到外都变得高效，没有任何浪费。

He could eat things that were vile, rotten, or hard to digest.

他可以吃恶心、腐烂或难以消化的东西。

Whatever he ate, his stomach used every last bit of value.

无论他吃什么，他的胃都会将其充分利用。

His blood carried the nutrients far through his powerful body.

他的血液将营养物质输送到他强健的身体各处。

This built strong tissues that gave him incredible endurance.

这使得他的组织变得强健，赋予他惊人的耐力。

His sight and smell became much more sensitive than before.

他的视觉和嗅觉比以前敏锐得多。

His hearing grew so sharp he could detect faint sounds in sleep.

他的听觉变得如此敏锐，以至于在睡眠中也能听见微弱的声音。

He knew in his dreams whether the sounds meant safety or danger.

他在梦中知道这些声音是意味着安全还是危险。

He learned to bite the ice between his toes with his teeth.

他学会了用牙齿咬脚趾间的冰。

If a water hole froze over, he would break the ice with his legs.

如果水坑结冰了，他就会用腿把冰破掉。

He reared up and struck the ice hard with stiff front limbs.

他直立起来，用僵硬的前肢用力撞击冰面。

His most striking ability was predicting wind changes overnight.

他最惊人的能力是预测一夜之间的风向变化。

Even when the air was still, he chose spots sheltered from wind.

即使空气静止时，他也会选择避风的地方。

Wherever he dug his nest, the next day's wind passed him by.

无论他在哪里筑巢，第二天的风都会吹过他。

He always ended up snug and protected, to leeward of the breeze.

他总是舒适地躲在下风处，受到保护。

Buck not only learned by experience—his instincts returned too.

巴克不仅通过经验学习，他的本能也恢复了。

The habits of domesticated generations began to fall away.

驯化一代人的习惯开始消失。

In vague ways, he remembered the ancient times of his breed.

他模糊地记得自己种族的古老时代。

He thought back to when wild dogs ran in packs through forests.

他回想起野狗成群结队地在森林里奔跑的情景。

They had chased and killed their prey while running it down.

他们在追捕猎物时追赶并杀死了猎物。

It was easy for Buck to learn how to fight with tooth and speed.

巴克很容易就学会了如何利用牙齿和速度进行战斗。

He used cuts, slashes, and quick snaps just like his ancestors.

他像他的祖先一样使用砍、砍和快速的折断。

Those ancestors stirred within him and awoke his wild nature.

那些祖先激起了他内心的骚动，唤醒了他狂野的本性。

Their old skills had passed into him through the bloodline.

他们的旧技能已通过血统传给了他。

Their tricks were his now, with no need for practice or effort.
现在他们的技巧已经为他所用，无需练习或努力。

On still, cold nights, Buck lifted his nose and howled.
在寂静寒冷的夜晚，巴克抬起鼻子嚎叫。
He howled long and deep, the way wolves had done long ago.
他发出一声深沉而悠长的嚎叫，就像很久以前的狼那样。
Through him, his dead ancestors pointed their noses and howled.
通过他，他死去的祖先们指着鼻子嚎叫。
They howled down through the centuries in his voice and shape.
它们以他的声音和身影，在几个世纪中一直咆哮。
His cadences were theirs, old cries that told of grief and cold.
他的歌声和他们的歌声一样，是诉说悲伤和寒冷的古老哭声。
They sang of darkness, of hunger, and the meaning of winter.
他们歌唱黑暗、饥饿和冬天的意义。
Buck proved of how life is shaped by forces beyond oneself,
巴克证明了生命是如何被超越自身的力量所塑造的，
the ancient song rose through Buck and took hold of his soul.
这首古老的歌谣在巴克心中回荡，并占据了他的灵魂。
He found himself because men had found gold in the North.
他找到了自己，因为人们在北方发现了黄金。
And he found himself because Manuel, the gardener's helper, needed money.
他之所以能找到自己，是因为园丁的助手曼努埃尔需要钱。

The Dominant Primordial Beast
主宰原始野兽

The dominant primordial beast was as strong as ever in Buck.
巴克身上占主导地位的原始野兽依然强大。

But the dominant primordial beast had lain dormant in him.
但那头占主导地位的原始野兽却在他体内沉睡。

Trail life was harsh, but it strengthened beast inside Buck.
越野生活虽然艰苦，但却增强了巴克内心的野兽之心。

Secretly the beast grew stronger and stronger every day.
野兽每天都在秘密地变得越来越强大。

But that inner growth stayed hidden to the outside world.
但内心的成长对于外界来说却是隐藏的。

A quiet and calm primordial force was building inside Buck.
一种安静而平和的原始力量正在巴克内心积聚。

New cunning gave Buck balance, calm control, and poise.
新的狡猾让巴克变得平衡、冷静、沉着。

Buck focused hard on adapting, never feeling fully relaxed.
巴克努力集中精力去适应，但始终感觉不到完全放松。

He avoided conflict, never starting fights, nor seeking trouble.
他避免冲突，从不挑起争斗，也不惹麻烦。

A slow, steady thoughtfulness shaped Buck's every move.
缓慢而稳定的深思熟虑塑造了巴克的每一个举动。

He avoided rash choices and sudden, reckless decisions.
他避免做出草率的选择和突然、鲁莽的决定。

Though Buck hated Spitz deeply, he showed him no aggression.
尽管巴克深恨斯皮茨，但他并没有向他表现出任何攻击性。

Buck never provoked Spitz, and kept his actions restrained.

巴克从未激怒过斯皮茨，并且保持着克制自己的行为。

Spitz, on the other hand, sensed the growing danger in Buck.

另一方面，斯皮茨感觉到巴克身上越来越大的危险。

He saw Buck as a threat and a serious challenge to his power.

他认为巴克是一个威胁，对他的权力是一个严峻的挑战。

He used every chance to snarl and show his sharp teeth.

他利用一切机会咆哮并露出锋利的牙齿。

He was trying to start the deadly fight that had to come.

他正试图发起一场必将到来的殊死战斗。

Early in the trip, a fight nearly broke out between them.

旅行初期，他们之间几乎爆发了一场争吵。

But an unexpected accident stopped the fight from happening.

但一场意外的事故阻止了这场战斗的发生。

That evening they set up camp on the bitterly cold Lake Le Barge.

那天晚上，他们在寒冷的勒巴尔日湖边扎营。

The snow was falling hard, and the wind cut like a knife.

雪下得很大，风像刀子一样刺骨。

The night had come too fast, and darkness surrounded them.

夜幕降临得太快，黑暗将他们包围。

They could hardly have chosen a worse place for rest.

他们选择的休息地点实在是太糟糕了。

The dogs searched desperately for a place to lie down.

狗拼命寻找一个可以躺下的地方。

A tall rock wall rose steeply behind the small group.

一堵高高的岩壁在这群人的身后陡然耸立。

The tent had been left behind in Dyea to lighten the load.

为了减轻负担，帐篷被留在了迪亚。

They had no choice but to make the fire on the ice itself.

他们别无选择，只能在冰上生火。

They spread their sleeping robes directly on the frozen lake.
他们把睡袍直接铺在冰冻的湖面上。

A few sticks of driftwood gave them a little bit of fire.
几根浮木为他们带来了一点火。

But the fire was built on the ice, and thawed through it.
但火是在冰上燃起的，并且通过冰融化。

Eventually they were eating their supper in darkness.
最后他们在黑暗中吃晚饭。

Buck curled up beside the rock, sheltered from the cold wind.
巴克蜷缩在岩石旁边，躲避寒风。

The spot was so warm and safe that Buck hated to move away.
这个地方非常温暖、安全，巴克不愿意离开。

But François had warmed the fish and was handing out rations.
但弗朗索瓦已经把鱼热好并分发了口粮。

Buck finished eating quickly, and returned to his bed.
巴克很快吃完饭，然后回到床上。

But Spitz was now laying where Buck had made his bed.
但斯皮茨现在正躺在巴克铺好床的地方。

A low snarl warned Buck that Spitz refused to move.
巴克低声咆哮着警告说，斯皮茨拒绝移动。

Until now, Buck had avoided this fight with Spitz.
到目前为止，巴克一直避免与斯皮茨发生战斗。

But deep inside Buck the beast finally broke loose.
但巴克内心深处的野兽终于挣脱了。

The theft of his sleeping place was too much to tolerate.
他的睡觉的地方被盗，这实在令人无法容忍。

Buck launched himself at Spitz, full of anger and rage.
巴克满怀愤怒和狂怒，向斯皮茨扑去。

Up until not Spitz had thought Buck was just a big dog.
直到现在，斯皮茨还以为巴克只是一只大狗。

He didn't think Buck had survived through his spirit.
他不认为巴克凭借其精神存活了下来。

He was expecting fear and cowardice, not fury and revenge.
他期待的是恐惧和懦弱，而不是愤怒和报复。

François stared as both dogs burst from the ruined nest.
弗朗索瓦目睹两只狗从被毁坏的狗窝里冲出来。

He understood at once what had started the wild struggle.
他立刻明白了是什么引发了这场激烈的争斗。

"A-a-ah!" François cried out in support of the brown dog.
"啊啊！"弗朗索瓦大声喊道，支持这只棕色的狗。

"Give him a beating! By God, punish that sneaky thief!"
"揍扁他！老天爷啊，惩罚一下这个鬼鬼祟祟的小偷！"

Spitz showed equal readiness and wild eagerness to fight.
斯皮茨表现出同样的准备和狂热的战斗热情。

He cried out in rage while circling fast, seeking an opening.
他一边愤怒地叫喊，一边快速地盘旋，寻找着突破口。

Buck showed the same hunger to fight, and the same caution.
巴克表现出同样的战斗渴望，以及同样的谨慎。

He circled his opponent as well, trying to gain the upper hand in battle.
他也绕着对手转圈，试图在战斗中占上风。

Then something unexpected happened and changed everything.
然后意想不到的事情发生了，改变了一切。

That moment delayed the eventual fight for the leadership.
那一刻推迟了最终的领导权之争。

Many miles of trail and struggle still waited before the end.
在终点之前，还有很长的路要走，还有许多艰辛等待着我们。

Perrault shouted an oath as a club smacked against bone.
当棍棒敲击骨头时，佩罗大声咒骂。

A sharp yelp of pain followed, then chaos exploded all around.

随后传来一声痛苦的尖叫，四周一片混乱。

Dark shapes moved in camp; wild huskies, starved and fierce.

营地里黑影移动；野性的哈士奇，饥饿而凶猛。

Four or five dozen huskies had sniffed the camp from far away.

四五十只哈士奇从远处嗅到了营地的气味。

They had crept in quietly while the two dogs fought nearby.

当两只狗在附近打架时，他们悄悄地潜了进来。

François and Perrault charged, swinging clubs at the invaders.

弗朗索瓦和佩罗发起冲锋，挥舞着棍棒向入侵者发起攻击。

The starving huskies showed teeth and fought back in frenzy.

饥饿的哈士奇露出牙齿，疯狂反击。

The smell of meat and bread had driven them past all fear.

肉和面包的香味驱散了他们的恐惧。

Perrault beat a dog that had buried its head in the grub-box.

佩罗殴打了一只把头埋在食物盒里的狗。

The blow hit hard, and the box flipped, food spilling out.

这一击很重，盒子翻转了，食物洒了出来。

In seconds, a score of wild beasts tore into the bread and meat.

几秒钟之内，二十只野兽就把面包和肉撕碎了。

The men's clubs landed blow after blow, but no dog turned away.

男人们的棍棒不断挥击，但没有一只狗能躲过。

They howled in pain, but fought until no food remained.

它们痛苦地嚎叫着，但仍在战斗，直到没有食物为止。

Meanwhile, the sled-dogs had jumped from their snowy beds.

与此同时，雪橇犬已经从雪床上跳了起来。

They were instantly attacked by the vicious hungry huskies.
他们立即遭到凶猛饥饿的哈士奇的袭击。

Buck had never seen such wild and starved creatures before.
巴克以前从未见过如此野蛮和饥饿的动物。

Their skin hung loose, barely hiding their skeletons.
他们的皮肤松弛下垂，几乎遮不住他们的骨骼。

There was a fire in their eyes, from hunger and madness
他们的眼睛里燃烧着饥饿和疯狂的火焰

There was no stopping them; no resisting their savage rush.
没有什么可以阻止他们；没有什么可以抵抗他们野蛮的冲锋。

The sled-dogs were shoved back, pressed against the cliff wall.
雪橇犬被推回，并被压在悬崖壁上。

Three huskies attacked Buck at once, tearing into his flesh.
三只哈士奇立刻向巴克发起攻击，撕咬他的肉体。

Blood poured from his head and shoulders, where he'd been cut.
他的头部和肩膀被割伤，鲜血直流。

The noise filled the camp; growling, yelps, and cries of pain.
营地里充满了噪音；咆哮声、尖叫声和痛苦的哭喊声。

Billee cried loudly, as usual, caught in the fray and panic.
比莉像往常一样，陷入了争斗和恐慌之中，大声哭了起来。

Dave and Solleks stood side by side, bleeding but defiant.
戴夫和索莱克斯并肩站着，浑身是血，但依然顽强抵抗。

Joe fought like a demon, biting anything that came close.
乔像恶魔一样战斗，咬任何靠近的东西。

He crushed a husky's leg with one brutal snap of his jaws.
他用嘴狠狠地咬碎了一只哈士奇的腿。

Pike jumped on the wounded husky and broke its neck instantly.

派克跳到受伤的哈士奇身上，瞬间扭断了它的脖子。

Buck caught a husky by the throat and ripped through the vein.

巴克抓住了哈士奇的喉咙并撕开了它的血管。

Blood sprayed, and the warm taste drove Buck into a frenzy.

鲜血喷洒而出，温热的味道让巴克陷入狂暴。

He hurled himself at another attacker without hesitation.

他毫不犹豫地向另一名袭击者扑去。

At the same moment, sharp teeth dug into Buck's own throat.

与此同时，锋利的牙齿咬住了巴克的喉咙。

Spitz had struck from the side, attacking without warning.

斯皮茨从侧面发起攻击，毫无预警。

Perrault and François had defeated the dogs stealing the food.

佩罗和弗朗索瓦打败了偷食物的狗。

Now they rushed to help their dogs fight back the attackers.

现在他们冲上前去帮助他们的狗反击袭击者。

The starving dogs retreated as the men swung their clubs.

当这些人挥动棍棒时，饥饿的狗纷纷撤退。

Buck broke free from the attack, but the escape was brief.

巴克挣脱了攻击，但逃脱的时间很短。

The men ran to save their dogs, and the huskies swarmed again.

男人们赶紧跑去救他们的狗，哈士奇们又蜂拥而至。

Billee, frightened into bravery, leapt into the pack of dogs.

比利吓得鼓起勇气，跳进了狗群。

But then he fled across the ice, in raw terror and panic.

但随后，他就惊恐万分，慌乱地穿过冰面逃走了。

Pike and Dub followed close behind, running for their lives.

派克和杜布紧随其后，逃命地奔跑。

The rest of the team broke and scattered, following after them.

其余队员也纷纷散开，跟在他们后面。

Buck gathered his strength to run, but then saw a flash.

巴克鼓起勇气准备跑，但突然看到一道闪光。

Spitz lunged at Buck's side, trying to knock him to the ground.

斯皮茨猛扑向巴克的侧面，试图将他击倒在地。

Under that mob of huskies, Buck would have had no escape.

在那群哈士奇的围剿下，巴克根本无法逃脱。

But Buck stood firm and braced for the blow from Spitz.

但巴克坚定地站着，准备迎接斯皮茨的打击。

Then he turned and ran out onto the ice with the fleeing team.

然后他转身和逃跑的队伍一起跑到了冰上。

Later, the nine sled-dogs gathered in the shelter of the woods.

随后，九只雪橇犬聚集在树林的掩蔽处。

No one chased them anymore, but they were battered and wounded.

没有人再追赶他们，但他们却伤痕累累。

Each dog had wounds; four or five deep cuts on every body.

每只狗都受伤了；每只狗身上都有四五处深深的伤口。

Dub had an injured hind leg and struggled to walk now.

杜布的后腿受伤了，现在走路很困难。

Dolly, the newest dog from Dyea, had a slashed throat.

多莉是戴亚家最新出生的狗，它的喉咙被割破了。

Joe had lost an eye, and Billee's ear was cut to pieces

乔失去了一只眼睛，比莉的耳朵被割成了碎片

All the dogs cried in pain and defeat through the night.

所有的狗都痛苦而沮丧地哭了一整夜。

At dawn they crept back to camp, sore and broken.

黎明时分，他们浑身伤痕累累，蹑手蹑脚地回到营地。

The huskies had vanished, but the damage had been done.
哈士奇消失了，但损失已经造成。

Perrault and François stood in foul moods over the ruin.
佩罗和弗朗索瓦站在废墟旁，心情十分沮丧。

Half of the food was gone, snatched by the hungry thieves.
一半的食物都没了，被饥饿的盗贼抢走了。

The huskies had torn through sled bindings and canvas.
哈士奇犬已经撕破了雪橇的绑带和帆布。

Anything with a smell of food had been devoured
completely.
任何有食物气味的东西都被吃光了。

They ate a pair of Perrault's moose-hide traveling boots.
他们吃了一双佩罗的驼鹿皮旅行靴。

They chewed leather reis and ruined straps beyond use.
它们啃咬皮革，损坏皮带，使其无法使用。

François stopped staring at the torn lash to check the dogs.
弗朗索瓦不再盯着被撕破的鞭子，而是去查看狗。

"Ah, my friends," he said, his voice low and filled with
worry.
"啊，我的朋友们，" 他低声说道，声音里充满了担
忧。

"Maybe all these bites will turn you into mad beasts."
"也许这些咬伤会让你们变成疯狂的野兽。"

"Maybe all mad dogs, sacredam! What do you think,
Perrault?"
"也许都是疯狗，天哪！你觉得怎么样，佩罗？"

Perrault shook his head, eyes dark with concern and fear.
佩罗摇了摇头，眼神里充满了担忧和恐惧。

Four hundred miles still lay between them and Dawson.
他们和道森之间仍有四百英里的距离。

Dog madness now could destroy any chance of survival.
现在，狗的疯狂可能会摧毁任何生存的机会。

They spent two hours swearing and trying to fix the gear.
他们花了两个小时咒骂并试图修复装备。

The wounded team finally left the camp, broken and defeated.
伤员队伍最终溃不成军，离开了营地。
This was the hardest trail yet, and each step was painful.
这是迄今为止最艰难的路程，每一步都很痛苦。
The Thirty Mile River had not frozen, and was rushing wildly.
三十里河尚未结冰，水流湍急。
Only in calm spots and swirling eddies did ice manage to hold.
只有在平静的地方和漩涡中冰才能保持稳定。
Six days of hard labor passed until the thirty miles were done.
经过六天的艰苦劳动，三十英里的路程终于完成了。
Each mile of the trail brought danger and the threat of death.
每英里的道路都带来危险和死亡的威胁。
The men and dogs risked their lives with every painful step.
男人和狗每走一步都冒着生命危险。
Perrault broke through thin ice bridges a dozen different times.
佩罗曾十几次打破薄冰桥。
He carried a pole and let it fall across the hole his body made.
他拿着一根杆子，让它落在他身体撞出的洞上。
More than once did that pole save Perrault from drowning.
这根杆子曾多次救佩罗免于溺水。
The cold snap held firm, the air was fifty degrees below zero.
寒流持续不断，气温降至零下五十度。
Every time he fell in, Perrault had to light a fire to survive.
每次掉下去，佩罗就必须点火才能生存。
Wet clothing froze fast, so he dried them near blazing heat.
湿衣服很快就结冻了，所以他用高温烘干它们。
No fear ever touched Perrault, and that made him a courier.
佩罗从不畏惧，这使他成为一名信使。

He was chosen for danger, and he met it with quiet resolve.
他被选中去承担危险，并且他以沉着的决心去面对它
。

He pressed forward into wind, his shriveled face frostbitten.
他迎风向前走去，干瘪的脸上满是冻伤。

From faint dawn to nightfall, Perrault led them onward.
从黎明微光到夜幕降临，佩罗带领他们继续前行。

He walked on narrow rim ice that cracked with every step.
他走在边缘狭窄的冰面上，每走一步，冰面都会裂开
。

They dared not stop—each pause risked a deadly collapse.
他们不敢停下来——
每一次停顿都有可能导致致命的崩溃。

One time the sled broke through, pulling Dave and Buck in.
有一次，雪橇冲破了雪道，把戴夫和巴克拉了进去。

By the time they were dragged free, both were near frozen.
当他们被拖出来时，两人都几乎冻僵了。

The men built a fire quickly to keep Buck and Dave alive.
男人们迅速生起火来，以保证巴克和戴夫活下去。

The dogs were coated in ice from nose to tail, stiff as carved
wood.
狗从鼻子到尾巴都覆盖着冰，僵硬得像雕刻的木头一
样。

The men ran them in circles near the fire to thaw their
bodies.
男人们让孩子们在火堆旁跑来跑去，以解冻孩子们的
尸体。

They came so close to the flames that their fur was singed.
它们距离火焰太近，以至于它们的皮毛都被烧焦了。

Spitz broke through the ice next, dragging in the team
behind him.
接下来，斯皮茨冲破了冰层，拖着身后的队伍。

The break reached all the way up to where Buck was
pulling.

断裂处一直延伸到巴克拉动的地方。

Buck leaned back hard, paws slipping and trembling on the edge.

巴克猛地向后靠去，爪子在边缘处打滑并颤抖。

Dave also strained backward, just behind Buck on the line.

戴夫也向后靠拢，刚好在巴克身后。

François hauled on the sled, his muscles cracking with effort.

弗朗索瓦拉着雪橇，他的肌肉因用力而发出嘎吱声。

Another time, rim ice cracked before and behind the sled.

还有一次，雪橇前后边缘的冰裂开了。

They had no way out except to climb a frozen cliff wall.

除了攀爬冰冻的悬崖壁外，他们没有其他出路。

Perrault somehow climbed the wall; a miracle kept him alive.

佩罗不知怎么地爬上了墙；奇迹让他活了下来。

François stayed below, praying for the same kind of luck.

弗朗索瓦留在楼下，祈祷着同样的好运。

They tied every strap, lashing, and trace into one long rope.

他们把每条皮带、捆扎带和牵引绳都绑成一根长绳。

The men hauled each dog up, one at a time to the top.

男人们把每只狗都拖上去，一次一只。

François climbed last, after the sled and the entire load.

弗朗索瓦（François）
最后一个爬上去，跟在雪橇和所有货物后面。

Then began a long search for a path down from the cliffs.

然后开始漫长的寻找从悬崖下来的道路。

They finally descended using the same rope they had made.

他们最终利用自己制作的同一根绳索下山。

Night fell as they returned to the riverbed, exhausted and sore.

当他们筋疲力尽、浑身酸痛地回到河床时，夜幕降临了。

They had taken a full day to cover only a quarter of a mile.

他们花了一整天的时间才走了四分之一英里。

By the time they reached the Hootalinqua, Buck was worn out.

当他们到达 Hootalinqua 时，巴克已经筋疲力尽了。

The other dogs suffered just as badly from the trail conditions.

其他狗也因路径状况而遭受了同样严重的伤害。

But Perrault needed to recover time, and pushed them on each day.

但佩罗需要恢复时间，并每天督促他们。

The first day they traveled thirty miles to Big Salmon.

第一天，他们行驶了三十英里到达大鲑鱼。

The next day they travelled thirty-five miles to Little Salmon.

第二天，他们行驶了三十五英里，到达了小萨蒙。

On the third day they pushed through forty long frozen miles.

第三天，他们走过了四十英里冰冻的路程。

By then, they were nearing the settlement of Five Fingers.

那时，他们已经接近五指定居点了。

Buck's feet were softer than the hard feet of native huskies.

巴克的脚比本地哈士奇的硬脚要柔软。

His paws had grown tender over many civilized generations.

经过多代文明的洗礼，他的爪子已经变得娇嫩。

Long ago, his ancestors had been tamed by river men or hunters.

很久以前，他的祖先被河人或猎人驯服了。

Every day Buck limped in pain, walking on raw, aching paws.

巴克每天都痛苦地跛行，用粗糙、疼痛的爪子行走。

At camp, Buck dropped like a lifeless form upon the snow.

在营地里，巴克像一个毫无生气的身影倒在雪地上。

Though starving, Buck did not rise to eat his evening meal.

尽管很饿，巴克还是没有起床吃晚饭。

François brought Buck his ration, laying fish by his muzzle.
弗朗索瓦给巴克送来了口粮，并把鱼放在巴克的嘴边。

Each night the driver rubbed Buck's feet for half an hour.
每天晚上，司机都会给巴克的脚揉半个小时。

François even cut up his own moccasins to make dog footwear.
弗朗索瓦甚至剪开自己的鹿皮鞋来制作狗鞋。

Four warm shoes gave Buck a great and welcome relief.
四双温暖的鞋子让巴克感到无比轻松。

One morning, François forgot the shoes, and Buck refused to rise.
一天早上，弗朗索瓦忘记了鞋子，而巴克拒绝起床。

Buck lay on his back, feet in the air, waving them pitifully.
巴克仰面躺着，双脚高高举起，可怜巴巴地挥舞着。

Even Perrault grinned at the sight of Buck's dramatic plea.
看到巴克戏剧性的恳求，就连佩罗也笑了。

Soon Buck's feet grew hard, and the shoes could be discarded.
很快，巴克的脚就变硬了，鞋子就可以扔掉了。

At Pelly, during harness time, Dolly let out a dreadful howl.
在佩利，当套上挽具时，多莉会发出一声可怕的嚎叫。

The cry was long and filled with madness, shaking every dog.
哭声悠长而疯狂，震得每只狗都颤抖起来。

Each dog bristled in fear without knowing the reason.
每只狗都不知道为什么而恐惧地竖起了毛。

Dolly had gone mad and hurled herself straight at Buck.
多莉已经疯了，她径直向巴克扑去。

Buck had never seen madness, but horror filled his heart.
巴克从未见过疯狂，但恐惧充满了他的内心。

With no thought, he turned and fled in absolute panic.

他没有多想，慌乱之中转身就逃。

Dolly chased him, her eyes wild, saliva flying from her jaws.

多莉追着他，眼神狂野，口水直流。

She kept right behind Buck, never gaining and never falling back.

她一直跟在巴克身后，既不前进，也不后退。

Buck ran through woods, down the island, across jagged ice.

巴克跑过树林，跑下小岛，跨过锯齿状的冰面。

He crossed to an island, then another, circling back to the river.

他穿过一座岛屿，然后又穿过另一座岛屿，绕回河边。

Still Dolly chased him, her growl close behind at every step.

多莉仍然追着他，每走一步，她都会在后面咆哮。

Buck could hear her breath and rage, though he dared not look back.

巴克可以听到她的呼吸和愤怒，尽管他不敢回头。

François shouted from afar, and Buck turned toward the voice.

弗朗索瓦从远处喊道，巴克顺着声音转过身。

Still gasping for air, Buck ran past, placing all hope in François.

巴克一边喘着气，一边跑过去，把所有的希望都寄托在弗朗索瓦身上。

The dog-driver raised an axe and waited as Buck flew past.

狗司机举起斧头，等待巴克飞奔而过。

The axe came down fast and struck Dolly's head with deadly force.

斧头迅速落下，致命一击击中了多莉的头部。

Buck collapsed near the sled, wheezing and unable to move.

巴克倒在雪橇旁，气喘吁吁，无法动弹。

That moment gave Spitz his chance to strike an exhausted foe.

那一刻，斯皮茨有机会攻击疲惫的敌人。

Twice he bit Buck, ripping flesh down to the white bone.

它两次咬了巴克，把肉撕成了白骨。

François's whip cracked, striking Spitz with full, furious force.

弗朗索瓦的鞭子啪的一声响起，用尽全力猛击斯皮茨。

Buck watched with joy as Spitz received his harshest beating yet.

巴克高兴地看着斯皮茨遭受迄今为止最惨痛的打击。

"He's a devil, that Spitz," Perrault muttered darkly to himself.

"那只斯皮茨犬真是个魔鬼，"佩罗阴沉地自言自语道。

"Someday soon, that cursed dog will kill Buck—I swear it."

"不久的将来，那条该死的狗会杀死巴克——我发誓。"

"That Buck has two devils in him," François replied with a nod.

"那只巴克心里有两个魔鬼，"弗朗索瓦点头回答道。

"When I watch Buck, I know something fierce waits in him."

"当我观察巴克时，我知道他内心深处隐藏着某种凶猛的东西。"

"One day, he'll get mad as fire and tear Spitz to pieces."

"总有一天，他会像火一样愤怒，把斯皮茨撕成碎片。"

"He'll chew that dog up and spit him on the frozen snow."

"他会把那只狗咬碎，然后把它吐在冰冻的雪地上。"

"Sure as anything, I know this deep in my bones."

"毫无疑问，我深知这一点。"

From that moment forward, the two dogs were locked in war.

从那一刻起，两只狗就开始互相争斗。

Spitz led the team and held power, but Buck challenged
that.
斯皮茨领导团队并掌握权力，但巴克对此提出了挑战
。

Spitz saw his rank threatened by this odd Southland
stranger.
斯皮茨发现他的地位受到了这个奇怪的南国陌生人的
威胁。

Buck was unlike any southern dog Spitz had known before.
巴克与斯皮兹以前认识的任何南方狗都不一样。

Most of them failed—too weak to live through cold and
hunger.
他们中的大多数人都失败了——
他们太虚弱了，无法忍受寒冷和饥饿。

They died fast under labor, frost, and the slow burn of
famine.
他们在劳作、霜冻和饥荒的缓慢侵蚀下迅速死去。

Buck stood apart—stronger, smarter, and more savage each
day.
巴克与众不同——他一天比一天强壮、聪明、凶猛。

He thrived on hardship, growing to match the northern
huskies.
他在艰苦中茁壮成长，最终成长为与北方哈士奇犬相
媲美的犬种。

Buck had strength, wild skill, and a patient, deadly instinct.
巴克拥有力量、野性、耐心和致命的本能。

The man with the club had beaten rashness out of Buck.
那个手持棍棒的人把巴克打得不再鲁莽了。

Blind fury was gone, replaced by quiet cunning and control.
盲目的愤怒消失了，取而代之的是安静的狡猾和控制
。

He waited, calm and primal, watching for the right moment.
他平静而原始地等待着，等待着合适的时机。

Their fight for command became unavoidable and clear.

他们争夺指挥权的斗争已变得不可避免且显而易见。

Buck desired leadership because his spirit demanded it.
巴克渴望成为领导者，因为他的精神需要它。

He was driven by the strange pride born of trail and harness.
他被源于小径和马具的奇特自豪感所驱使。

That pride made dogs pull till they collapsed on the snow.
那种骄傲让狗一直拖着，直到倒在雪地上。

Pride lured them into giving all the strength they had.
骄傲引诱他们付出所有的力量。

Pride can lure a sled-dog even to the point of death.
骄傲甚至会引诱雪橇犬走向死亡。

Losing the harness left dogs broken and without purpose.
失去挽具会让狗变得残废，失去生存的意义。

The heart of a sled-dog can be crushed by shame when they retire.
当雪橇犬退役时，它的心可能会因羞愧而破碎。

Dave lived by that pride as he dragged the sled from behind.
戴夫在后面拖着雪橇，活出了那种自豪感。

Solleks, too, gave his all with grim strength and loyalty.
索莱克斯也以坚定的力量和忠诚奉献了自己的一切。

Each morning, pride turned them from bitter to determined.
每天早晨，骄傲都会让他们从痛苦变得坚定。

They pushed all day, then dropped silent at the camp's end.
他们奋力前进了一整天，然后安静地走到营地的尽头。

That pride gave Spitz the strength to beat shirkers into line.
正是这份骄傲让斯皮茨有力量打败那些逃避责任的人。

Spitz feared Buck because Buck carried that same deep pride.
斯皮茨害怕巴克，因为巴克也怀有同样的深沉自尊。

Buck's pride now stirred against Spitz, and he did not stop.
巴克的自尊心现在对斯皮茨产生了反感，他没有停下来。

Buck defied Spitz's power and blocked him from punishing dogs.

巴克违抗斯皮茨的权力并阻止他惩罚狗。

When others failed, Buck stepped between them and their leader.

当其他人失败时，巴克便介入他们与他们的领袖之间。

He did this with intent, making his challenge open and clear.

他有意这样做，使他的挑战变得公开而明确。

On one night heavy snow blanketed the world in deep silence.

一天晚上，大雪覆盖，世界陷入深深的寂静。

The next morning, Pike, lazy as ever, did not rise for work.

第二天早上，派克还是像往常一样懒惰，没有起床去上班。

He stayed hidden in his nest beneath a thick layer of snow.

他藏在厚厚的积雪下的巢穴里。

François called out and searched, but could not find the dog.

弗朗索瓦大声呼喊并四处寻找，但没能找到那只狗。

Spitz grew furious and stormed through the snow-covered camp.

斯皮茨勃然大怒，冲进了白雪覆盖的营地。

He growled and sniffed, digging madly with blazing eyes.

他咆哮着，嗅着，眼睛闪着光，疯狂地挖掘着。

His rage was so fierce that Pike shook under the snow in fear.

他的愤怒是如此强烈，以至于派克吓得在雪下颤抖。

When Pike was finally found, Spitz lunged to punish the hiding dog.

当终于找到派克时，斯皮茨猛扑过去，惩罚这只躲藏的狗。

But Buck sprang between them with a fury equal to Spitz's own.

但巴克突然冲到他们中间，其愤怒与斯皮茨不相上下。

The attack was so sudden and clever that Spitz fell off his feet.
这次攻击是如此突然和巧妙，以至于斯皮茨摔倒了。

Pike, who had been shaking, took courage from this defiance.
派克原本浑身颤抖，但这次反抗让他鼓起了勇气。

He leapt on the fallen Spitz, following Buck's bold example.
他学着巴克的大胆举动，跳到了倒下的斯皮茨犬身上。

Buck, no longer bound by fairness, joined the strike on Spitz.
巴克不再受公平的约束，加入了对斯皮茨的攻击。

François, amused yet firm in discipline, swung his heavy lash.
弗朗索瓦感到很有趣，但仍然坚持纪律，挥舞着沉重的鞭子。

He struck Buck with all his strength to break up the fight.
他用尽全力击打巴克，以阻止这场打斗。

Buck refused to move and stayed atop the fallen leader.
巴克拒绝移动，留在倒下的领袖身上。

François then used the whip's handle, hitting Buck hard.
然后弗朗索瓦用鞭子柄狠狠地抽了巴克。

Staggering from the blow, Buck fell back under the assault.
巴克被击中后摇摇晃晃，在攻击下倒下了。

François struck again and again while Spitz punished Pike.
弗朗索瓦一次又一次发起攻击，而斯皮茨则惩罚派克。

Days passed, and Dawson City grew nearer and nearer.
日子一天天过去，道森城越来越近了。

Buck kept interfering, slipping between Spitz and other dogs.

巴克不断干扰，在斯皮茨和其他狗之间穿梭。

He chose his moments well, always waiting for François to leave.

他选择时机很好，总是等待弗朗索瓦离开。

Buck's quiet rebellion spread, and disorder took root in the team.

巴克的静默反抗蔓延开来，队伍中陷入混乱。

Dave and Solleks stayed loyal, but others grew unruly.

戴夫和索莱克斯依然忠诚，但其他人却变得不守规矩。

The team grew worse—restless, quarrelsome, and out of line.

团队变得越来越糟糕——
焦躁不安、争吵不断、不守规矩。

Nothing worked smoothly anymore, and fights became common.

一切都不再顺利，争斗变得频繁起来。

Buck stayed at the heart of the trouble, always provoking unrest.

巴克始终处于麻烦的中心，总是挑起动乱。

François stayed alert, afraid of the fight between Buck and Spitz.

弗朗索瓦保持警惕，害怕巴克和斯皮茨之间的打斗。

Each night, scuffles woke him, fearing the beginning finally arrived.

每个晚上，打斗声都会把他吵醒，他担心战争的开始终于到来了。

He leapt from his robe, ready to break up the fight.

他从长袍中跳起来，准备阻止这场争斗。

But the moment never came, and they reached Dawson at last.

但这一刻并没有到来，他们最终到达了道森。

The team entered the town one bleak afternoon, tense and quiet.

一个阴冷的下午，队伍进入了小镇，气氛紧张而安静。

The great battle for leadership still hung in the frozen air.
争夺领导权的激烈斗争仍然悬而未决。

Dawson was full of men and sled-dogs, all busy with work.
道森到处都是忙于工作的人们和雪橇犬。

Buck watched the dogs pull loads from morning until night.
巴克从早到晚看着狗拉着货物。

They hauled logs and firewood, freighted supplies to the mines.
他们运送原木和木柴，将物资运送到矿井。

Where horses once worked in the Southland, dogs now labored.
南方地区曾经靠马匹劳作，而现在则由狗来干活。

Buck saw some dogs from the South, but most were wolf-like huskies.
巴克看到了一些来自南方的狗，但大多数是像狼一样的哈士奇。

At night, like clockwork, the dogs raised their voices in song.
入夜后，就像时钟一样，狗儿们开始放声歌唱。

At nine, at midnight, and again at three, the singing began.
九点、午夜、三点，歌声再次响起。

Buck loved joining their eerie chant, wild and ancient in sound.
巴克喜欢加入他们那狂野而古老的怪诞吟唱。

The aurora flamed, stars danced, and snow blanketed the land.
极光闪耀，繁星闪烁，白雪覆盖大地。

The dogs' song rose as a cry against silence and bitter cold.
狗的歌声响起，是对寂静和严寒的呐喊。

But their howl held sorrow, not defiance, in every long note.
但他们的嚎叫声中，每一个长音都带着悲伤，而不是反抗。

Each wailing cry was full of pleading; the burden of life itself.

每一声哀号都充满着恳求；充满着生命本身的重担。

That song was old—older than towns, and older than fires

这首歌很古老——比城镇更古老，比火更古老

That song was more ancient even than the voices of men.

那首歌甚至比人类的声音还要古老。

It was a song from the young world, when all songs were sad.

这是一首来自年轻世界的歌曲，那时所有的歌曲都是悲伤的。

The song carried sorrow from countless generations of dogs.

这首歌承载着无数代狗狗的悲伤。

Buck felt the melody deeply, moaning from pain rooted in the ages.

巴克深深地感受着这旋律，因根植于岁月的痛苦而呻吟。

He sobbed from a grief as old as the wild blood in his veins.

他因悲伤而抽泣，这种悲伤就像他血管里狂野的血液一样古老。

The cold, the dark, and the mystery touched Buck's soul.

寒冷、黑暗和神秘触动了巴克的灵魂。

That song proved how far Buck had returned to his origins.

那首歌证明了巴克已经回归到他的本源有多远。

Through snow and howling he had found the start of his own life.

在冰雪和嚎叫中，他找到了自己生命的起点。

Seven days after arriving in Dawson, they set off once again.

抵达道森七天后，他们再次出发。

The team dropped from the Barracks down to the Yukon Trail.

队伍从军营出发，前往育空小道。

They began the journey back toward Dyea and Salt Water.

他们开始返回戴亚和盐水镇的旅程。

Perrault carried dispatches even more urgent than before.
佩罗传递的急件比以前更加紧急。

He was also seized by trail pride and aimed to set a record.
他也对越野跑感到自豪，并立志要创造一项纪录。

This time, several advantages were on Perrault's side.
这一次，佩罗一方占据了多项优势。

The dogs had rested for a full week and regained their strength.
狗狗们休息了整整一周，恢复了体力。

The trail they had broken was now hard-packed by others.
他们开辟出来的小路现在已被其他人踩踏殆尽。

In places, police had stored food for dogs and men alike.
在一些地方，警察为狗和人储存了食物。

Perrault traveled light, moving fast with little to weigh him down.
佩罗轻装出行，行动迅速，几乎没有什么负担。

They reached Sixty-Mile, a fifty-mile run, by the first night.
第一天晚上，他们就跑到了六十英里，也就是五十英里。

On the second day, they rushed up the Yukon toward Pelly.
第二天，他们沿着育空河向佩利进发。

But such fine progress came with much strain for François.
但如此好的进步也给弗朗索瓦带来了很大的压力。

Buck's quiet rebellion had shattered the team's discipline.
巴克的无声反抗破坏了球队的纪律。

They no longer pulled together like one beast in the reins.
他们不再像一头野兽一样齐心协力。

Buck had led others into defiance through his bold example.
巴克以他大胆的榜样带领其他人走向反抗。

Spitz's command was no longer met with fear or respect.
斯皮茨的命令不再受到恐惧或尊重。

The others lost their awe of him and dared to resist his rule.
其他人不再敬畏他，并敢于反抗他的统治。

One night, Pike stole half a fish and ate it under Buck's eye.
一天晚上，派克偷了半条鱼并在巴克的眼皮底下吃了它。

Another night, Dub and Joe fought Spitz and went unpunished.
另一天晚上，杜布和乔与斯皮茨打斗，但并未受到惩罚。

Even Billee whined less sweetly and showed new sharpness.
甚至连比莉的哀嚎也不再那么甜美，反而显得尖刻起来。

Buck snarled at Spitz every time they crossed paths.
每次与斯皮茨相遇，巴克都会对它咆哮。

Buck's attitude grew bold and threatening, nearly like a bully.
巴克的态度变得大胆而具有威胁性，几乎就像一个恶霸。

He paced before Spitz with a swagger, full of mocking menace.
他大摇大摆地在斯皮茨面前踱步，眼神里充满了嘲讽和威胁。

That collapse of order also spread among the sled-dogs.
秩序的崩溃也蔓延到了雪橇犬之中。

They fought and argued more than ever, filling camp with noise.
他们打架、争吵比以前更加频繁，营地里充满了噪音。

Camp life turned into a wild, howling chaos each night.
营地生活每晚都变得狂野、混乱。

Only Dave and Solleks remained steady and focused.
只有戴夫和索莱克斯保持稳定和专注。

But even they became short-tempered from the constant brawls.
但即使如此，他们也因不断的争吵而变得脾气暴躁。

François cursed in strange tongues and stomped in frustration.
弗朗索瓦用奇怪的语言咒骂，并沮丧地跺脚。

He tore at his hair and shouted while snow flew underfoot.
他一边扯着头发，一边大声喊叫，脚下雪花飞舞。

His whip snapped across the pack but barely kept them in line.
他的鞭子抽打着马群，但几乎没有让它们保持队形。

Whenever his back was turned, the fighting broke out again.
每当他转身，战斗就会再次爆发。

François used the lash for Spitz, while Buck led the rebels.
弗朗索瓦用鞭子抽打斯皮茨，而巴克则领导叛军。

Each knew the other's role, but Buck avoided any blame.
每个人都知道对方的角色，但巴克避免承担任何责任。

François never caught Buck starting a fight or shirking his job.
弗朗索瓦从未发现巴克挑起打架或逃避工作。

Buck worked hard in harness—the toil now thrilled his spirit.
巴克在马具上辛勤劳作——
现在，辛劳让他精神振奋。

But he found even more joy in stirring fights and chaos in camp.
但他发现在营地里挑起争斗和混乱更让他开心。

At the Tahkeena's mouth one evening, Dub startled a rabbit.
一天晚上，在塔基纳（Tahkeena）的嘴边，杜布（Dub）惊吓到了一只兔子。

He missed the catch, and the snowshoe rabbit sprang away.
他没能抓住雪鞋兔，而雪鞋兔也逃走了。

In seconds, the entire sled team gave chase with wild cries.
几秒钟之内，整个雪橇队就发出狂野的叫喊声追了上去。

Nearby, a Northwest Police camp housed fifty husky dogs.
附近的西北警察营地里饲养了五十只哈士奇犬。

They joined the hunt, surging down the frozen river together.
他们加入了狩猎，一起顺着冰冻的河流前进。

The rabbit turned off the river, fleeing up a frozen creek bed.
兔子离开河流，沿着结冰的河床逃走。

The rabbit skipped lightly over snow while the dogs struggled through.
兔子在雪地上轻轻跳跃，而狗则艰难地穿过雪地。

Buck led the massive pack of sixty dogs around each twisting bend.
巴克带领着这群由六十条狗组成的庞大狗群绕过每一个弯道。

He pushed forward, low and eager, but could not gain ground.
他低着头，急切地向前推进，但却无法取得进展。

His body flashed under the pale moon with each powerful leap.
每一次有力的跳跃，他的身躯都在苍白的月光下闪动。

Ahead, the rabbit moved like a ghost, silent and too fast to catch.
前方，兔子像幽灵一样移动，悄无声息，速度快得难以捕捉。

All those old instincts—the hunger, the thrill—rushed through Buck.
所有这些旧本能——饥饿、刺激——
都涌入巴克的心中。

Humans feel this instinct at times, driven to hunt with gun and bullet.
人类有时会感受到这种本能，驱使人们用枪和子弹去狩猎。

But Buck felt this feeling on a deeper and more personal level.
但巴克在更深层次、更个人的层面上感受到了这种感觉。

They could not feel the wild in their blood the way Buck could feel it.
他们无法像巴克那样感受到血液中的野性。

He chased living meat, ready to kill with his teeth and taste blood.
他追逐活肉，准备用牙齿杀死并品尝鲜血。

His body strained with joy, wanting to bathe in warm red life.
他的身体因喜悦而紧绷，想要沐浴在温暖的红色生命中。

A strange joy marks the highest point life can ever reach.
奇异的喜悦标志着生命所能达到的最高点。

The feeling of a peak where the living forget they are even alive.
巅峰之感让活着的人忘记自己还活着。

This deep joy touches the artist lost in blazing inspiration.
这种深深的喜悦，感动了沉浸在炽热灵感中的艺术家。

This joy seizes the soldier who fights wildly and spares no foe.
这种喜悦抓住了那些疯狂战斗、不放过任何敌人的士兵。

This joy now claimed Buck as he led the pack in primal hunger.
这种快乐现在占据了巴克的心灵，因为他在原始饥饿中带领着狼群。

He howled with the ancient wolf-cry, thrilled by the living chase.
他发出古老的狼嚎，为这场活生生的追逐而兴奋不已。

Buck tapped into the oldest part of himself, lost in the wild.

巴克挖掘出了自己最古老的部分，迷失在荒野之中。

He reached deep within, past memory, into raw, ancient time.

他深入内心，回忆过去，进入原始的远古时代。

A wave of pure life surged through every muscle and tendon.

一股纯净的生命之波，涌遍全身肌肉和肌腱。

Each leap shouted that he lived, that he moved through death.

他的每一次跳跃都宣告着他活着，他穿越了死亡。

His body soared joyfully over still, cold land that never stirred.

他的身体欢快地飞越那片静止、冰冷、从未动静的土地。

Spitz stayed cold and cunning, even in his wildest moments.

即使在最疯狂的时刻，斯皮茨也保持着冷静和狡猾。

He left the trail and crossed land where the creek curved wide.

他离开小路，穿过小溪弯曲的土地。

Buck, unaware of this, stayed on the rabbit's winding path.

巴克对此毫不知情，继续沿着兔子蜿蜒的小路走着。

Then, as Buck rounded a bend, the ghost-like rabbit was before him.

然后，当巴克转过一个弯道时，那只幽灵般的兔子出现在他面前。

He saw a second figure leap from the bank ahead of the prey.

他看到第二个身影从河岸上跃起，跑到了猎物的前面。

The figure was Spitz, landing right in the path of the fleeing rabbit.

那个身影正是斯皮茨，它正好落在了逃跑的兔子的路径上。

The rabbit could not turn and met Spitz's jaws in mid-air.

兔子无法转身，在半空中撞上了斯皮茨的下巴。

The rabbit's spine broke with a shriek as sharp as a dying human's cry.

兔子的脊椎断裂了，发出一声如同人类濒死哀嚎般的尖叫。

At that sound—the fall from life to death—the pack howled loud.

听到那声音——从生到死的坠落——
狼群发出了大声的嚎叫。

A savage chorus rose from behind Buck, full of dark delight.

巴克身后响起一阵狂野的合唱，充满阴暗的喜悦。

Buck gave no cry, no sound, and charged straight into Spitz.

巴克没有叫喊，没有发出任何声音，径直向斯皮茨冲去。

He aimed for the throat, but struck the shoulder instead.

他瞄准的是喉咙，但却击中了肩膀。

They tumbled through soft snow; their bodies locked in combat.

他们在柔软的雪地上翻滚；他们的身体扭打在一起。

Spitz sprang up quickly, as if never knocked down at all.

斯皮茨迅速跳起，仿佛根本就没有被击倒过一样。

He slashed Buck's shoulder, then leaped clear of the fight.

他砍伤了巴克的肩膀，然后跳开了战斗。

Twice his teeth snapped like steel traps, lips curled and fierce.

他的牙齿像钢陷阱一样咬合了两次，嘴唇猛地卷起。

He backed away slowly, seeking firm ground under his feet.

他慢慢地后退，寻找脚下坚实的地面。

Buck understood the moment instantly and fully.

巴克立刻就完全理解了这一刻。

The time had come; the fight was going to be a fight to the death.

时机已到，这场战斗将是一场你死我活的战斗。

The two dogs circled, growling, ears flat, eyes narrowed.

两只狗绕着圈子，咆哮着，耳朵放平，眼睛眯成一条缝。

Each dog waited for the other to show weakness or misstep.
每只狗都在等待另一只狗表现出软弱或失误。

To Buck, the scene felt eerily known and deeply remembered.
对于巴克来说，这个场景感觉异常熟悉，并且记忆深刻。

The white woods, the cold earth, the battle under moonlight.
白色的树林，冰冷的大地，月光下的战斗。

A heavy silence filled the land, deep and unnatural.
大地上弥漫着一种沉重的寂静，深沉而不自然。

No wind stirred, no leaf moved, no sound broke the stillness.
没有风吹拂，没有树叶摇动，没有任何声音打破寂静。

The dogs' breaths rose like smoke in the frozen, quiet air.
狗的呼吸在冰冷、寂静的空气中像烟雾一样升起。

The rabbit was long forgotten by the pack of wild beasts.
这只兔子早已被野兽群遗忘了。

These half-tamed wolves now stood still in a wide circle.
这些半驯服的狼此刻站成一个大圆圈。

They were quiet, only their glowing eyes revealed their hunger.
它们安静下来，只有闪闪发光的眼睛透露出饥饿感。

Their breath drifted upward, watching the final fight begin.
他们的呼吸向上飘荡，看着最后的战斗开始。

To Buck, this battle was old and expected, not strange at all.
对于巴克来说，这场战斗早已习以为常，毫无陌生感。

It felt like a memory of something always meant to happen.
这感觉就像是注定要发生的事情的记忆。

Spitz was a trained fighting dog, honed by countless wild brawls.

斯皮茨是一只经过训练的斗犬，经过无数次野外斗殴的磨练。

From Spitzbergen to Canada, he had mastered many foes.
从斯匹次卑尔根到加拿大，他战胜了许多敌人。

He was filled with fury, but never gave control to rage.
他心中充满愤怒，但却从不控制自己的愤怒。

His passion was sharp, but always tempered by hard instinct.
他的热情很强烈，但总是受到坚强本能的缓和。

He never attacked until his own defense was in place.
在他自己的防御到位之前，他绝不会发起攻击。

Buck tried again and again to reach Spitz's vulnerable neck.
巴克一次又一次地尝试去够斯皮茨脆弱的脖子。

But every strike was met by a slash from Spitz's sharp teeth.
但每一次攻击都会被斯皮茨锋利的牙齿咬住。

Their fangs clashed, and both dogs bled from torn lips.
它们的尖牙相撞，两只狗的嘴唇都被撕裂，鲜血直流。

No matter how Buck lunged, he couldn't break the defense.
无论巴克如何猛扑，都无法突破防守。

He grew more furious, rushing in with wild bursts of power.
他越发愤怒，爆发出狂野的力量冲了进来。

Again and again, Buck struck for the white throat of Spitz.
巴克一次又一次地攻击斯皮茨的白色喉咙。

Each time Spitz evaded and struck back with a slicing bite.
每次 Spitz 都会躲避并以猛烈的咬击进行反击。

Then Buck shifted tactics, rushing as if for the throat again.
然后巴克改变了策略，再次冲向喉咙。

But he pulled back mid-attack, turning to strike from the side.
但他在进攻中途撤退，转身从侧面发起攻击。

He threw his shoulder into Spitz, aiming to knock him down.
他用肩膀撞向斯皮茨，想将他击倒。

Each time he tried, Spitz dodged and countered with a slash.
每次他尝试，斯皮茨都会躲开并用砍刀反击。
Buck's shoulder grew raw as Spitz leapt clear after every hit.
每次击中斯皮茨后，他都会跳起来，而巴克的肩膀则变得疼痛。
Spitz had not been touched, while Buck bled from many wounds.
斯皮茨毫发无损，而巴克却多处受伤流血。
Buck's breath came fast and heavy, his body slick with blood.
巴克的呼吸急促而沉重，他的身上沾满了鲜血。
The fight turned more brutal with each bite and charge.
随着每一次咬伤和冲锋，战斗变得更加残酷。
Around them, sixty silent dogs waited for the first to fall.
在它们周围，六十只狗静静地等待着第一只狗倒下。
If one dog dropped, the pack were going to finish the fight.
只要有一只狗倒下，整群狗就会结束这场战斗。
Spitz saw Buck weakening, and began to press the attack.
斯皮茨看到巴克逐渐虚弱，便开始发起攻击。
He kept Buck off balance, forcing him to fight for footing.
他让巴克失去平衡，迫使他奋力站立。
Once Buck stumbled and fell, and all the dogs rose up.
有一次，巴克绊倒了，所有的狗都站了起来。
But Buck righted himself mid-fall, and everyone sank back down.
但巴克在下落过程中恢复了平衡，所有人都再次沉了下去。
Buck had something rare—imagination born from deep instinct.
巴克拥有一种罕见的东西——
源于深层本能的想象力。
He fought by natural drive, but he also fought with cunning.
他凭借天生的斗志战斗，但也凭借狡猾的手段战斗。
He charged again as if repeating his shoulder attack trick.

他再次冲锋，仿佛在重复他的肩部攻击技巧。

But at the last second, he dropped low and swept beneath Spitz.

但在最后一秒，他俯冲下来并从斯皮茨下方掠过。

His teeth locked on Spitz's front left leg with a snap.

他的牙齿猛地咬住了斯皮茨的左前腿。

Spitz now stood unsteady, his weight on only three legs.

斯皮茨现在站不稳，他的体重只靠三条腿支撑。

Buck struck again, tried three times to bring him down.

巴克再次发起攻击，三次试图将他击倒。

On the fourth attempt he used the same move with success

第四次尝试时，他使用同样的动作成功了

This time Buck managed to bite the right leg of Spitz.

这次巴克成功咬住了斯皮茨的右腿。

Spitz, though crippled and in agony, kept struggling to survive.

斯皮茨虽然残疾且痛苦不堪，但仍在为生存而努力奋斗。

He saw the circle of huskies tighten, tongues out, eyes glowing.

他看到一群哈士奇围成一圈，舌头伸出，眼睛闪闪发光。

They waited to devour him, just as they had done to others.

他们等着吞噬他，就像他们对其他人所做的那样。

This time, he stood in the center; defeated and doomed.

这一次，他站在了中心，失败了，注定要失败。

There was no option to escape for the white dog now.

白狗现在已经没有逃跑的选择。

Buck showed no mercy, for mercy did not belong in the wild.

巴克毫不留情，因为野性中不存在怜悯。

Buck moved carefully, setting up for the final charge.

巴克小心翼翼地移动，准备发起最后的冲锋。

The circle of huskies closed in; he felt their warm breaths.

哈士奇们围成一圈，他感觉到它们温暖的呼吸。

They crouched low, prepared to spring when the moment came.

他们蹲下身子，准备在时机成熟时跳起。

Spitz quivered in the snow, snarling and shifting his stance.

斯皮茨在雪地里颤抖着，咆哮着，不断改变着姿势。

His eyes glared, lips curled, teeth flashing in desperate threat.

他双眼怒视，嘴唇撇着，露出牙齿，露出绝望的威胁表情。

He staggered, still trying to hold off the cold bite of death.

他跟跄着，仍然试图抵挡死亡的冰冷咬咬。

He had seen this before, but always from the winning side.

他以前也见过这种情况，但总是从胜利者的角度看。

Now he was on the losing side; the defeated; the prey; death.

现在他站在了失败的一方；被击败的一方；猎物；死亡的一方。

Buck circled for the final blow, the ring of dogs pressed closer.

巴克绕圈准备发动最后一击，而狗群则围得更紧了。

He could feel their hot breaths; ready for the kill.

他能感觉到他们灼热的呼吸；准备杀戮。

A stillness fell; all was in its place; time had stopped.

一切都安静下来；一切都恢复了原状；时间停止了。

Even the cold air between them froze for one last moment.

就连两人之间冰冷的空气，也在最后一刻凝固了。

Only Spitz moved, trying to hold off his bitter end.

只有斯皮茨还在动，试图阻止自己走向痛苦的结局。

The circle of dogs was closing in around him, as was his destiny.

一群狗正在向他逼近，他的命运也随之终结。

He was desperate now, knowing what was about to happen.

他现在很绝望，知道即将发生什么。

Buck sprang in, shoulder met shoulder one last time.

巴克跳了进来，最后一次肩膀碰了碰。

The dogs surged forward, covering Spitz in the snowy dark.
狗群猛扑上前，将斯皮茨笼罩在雪白的黑暗之中。

Buck watched, standing tall; the victor in a savage world.
巴克昂首挺胸地注视着这一切；他是野蛮世界中的胜利者。

The dominant primordial beast had made its kill, and it was good.
占主导地位的原始野兽已经杀死了猎物，这很好。

He, Who Has Won to Mastership
他，赢得了大师的地位

"Eh? What did I say? I speak true when I say Buck is a devil."

"呃？我说什么了？我说巴克是个魔鬼，这话可是对的。"

François said this the next morning after finding Spitz missing.

第二天早上，弗朗索瓦发现斯皮茨失踪后说了这句话。

Buck stood there, covered with wounds from the vicious fight.

巴克站在那里，浑身是激烈打斗造成的伤口。

François pulled Buck near the fire and pointed at the injuries.

弗朗索瓦把巴克拉到火堆旁，指着伤口。

"That Spitz fought like the Devik," said Perrault, eyeing the deep gashes.

"那只斯皮茨的战斗力就像德维克一样，"佩罗看着深深的伤口说道。

"And that Buck fought like two devils," François replied at once.

"巴克打起来就像两个魔鬼一样，"弗朗索瓦立刻回答道。

"Now we will make good time; no more Spitz, no more trouble."

"现在我们可以顺利度过，不再有斯皮茨，不再有麻烦了。"

Perrault was packing the gear and loaded the sled with care.

佩罗正在打包装备并小心翼翼地装载雪橇。

François harnessed the dogs in preparation for the day's run.

弗朗索瓦给狗套上挽具，为一天的奔跑做准备。

Buck trotted straight to the lead position once held by Spitz.

巴克径直小跑到斯皮茨曾经占据的领先位置。

But François, not noticing, led Solleks forward to the front.
但弗朗索瓦没有注意到，带领索莱克斯走向了前线。

In François's judgment, Solleks was now the best lead-dog.
在弗朗索瓦看来，索莱克斯现在是最好的领头犬。

Buck sprang at Solleks in fury and drove him back in protest.
巴克愤怒地向索莱克斯扑去，并把他赶了回去以示抗议。

He stood where Spitz once had stood, claiming the lead position.
他站在斯皮茨曾经站过的地方，占据领先位置。

"Eh? Eh?" cried François, slapping his thighs in amusement.
"啊？啊？" 弗朗索瓦叫道，高兴地拍着大腿。

"Look at Buck—he killed Spitz, now he wants to take the job!"
"看看巴克——
他杀了斯皮茨，现在他想接手这份工作！"

"Go away, Chook!" he shouted, trying to drive Buck away.
"走开，Chook！" 他大喊，试图把巴克赶走。

But Buck refused to move and stood firm in the snow.
但巴克拒绝移动，坚定地站在雪地里。

François grabbed Buck by the scruff, dragging him aside.
弗朗索瓦抓住巴克的颈背，把他拖到一边。

Buck growled low and threateningly but did not attack.
巴克低声发出威胁性的咆哮声，但并没有发起攻击。

François put Solleks back in the lead, trying to settle the dispute
弗朗索瓦让索莱克斯重新领先，试图解决争端

The old dog showed fear of Buck and didn't want to stay.
老狗对巴克表现出恐惧，不想留下来。

When François turned his back, Buck drove Solleks out again.
当弗朗索瓦转身时，巴克再次把索莱克斯赶了出去。

Solleks did not resist and quietly stepped aside once more.
索莱克斯没有反抗，再次悄悄地走到了一边。

François grew angry and shouted, "By God, I fix you!"
弗朗索瓦非常生气，大声喊道："上帝啊，我要解决掉你！"

He came toward Buck holding a heavy club in his hand.
他手里拿着一根沉重的棍棒向巴克走来。

Buck remembered the man in the red sweater well.
巴克清楚地记得那个穿红毛衣的男人。

He retreated slowly, watching François, but growling deeply.
他慢慢地后退，注视着弗朗索瓦，但发出低沉的咆哮声。

He did not rush back, even when Solleks stood in his place.
即使索莱克斯站在他的位置上，他也没有急忙后退。

Buck circled just beyond reach, snarling in fury and protest.
巴克在它够不着的地方绕了一圈，愤怒地咆哮着表示抗议。

He kept his eyes on the club, ready to dodge if François threw.
他一直盯着球杆，准备在弗朗索瓦扔球时躲避。

He had grown wise and wary in the ways of men with weapons.
他已经变得聪明并且对持有武器的人的行为更加谨慎。

François gave up and called Buck to his former place again.
弗朗索瓦放弃了，再次把巴克叫到原来的地方。

But Buck stepped back cautiously, refusing to obey the order.
但巴克小心翼翼地后退，拒绝服从命令。

François followed, but Buck only retreated a few steps more.
弗朗索瓦跟了上去，但巴克只是后退了几步。

After some time, François threw the weapon down in frustration.

过了一会儿，弗朗索瓦沮丧地扔掉了武器。

He thought Buck feared a beating and was going to come quietly.

他以为巴克害怕挨打，所以会悄悄地走过去。

But Buck wasn't avoiding punishment—he was fighting for rank.

但巴克并没有逃避惩罚——他是在为地位而战。

He had earned the lead-dog spot through a fight to the death

他通过一场殊死搏斗赢得了领头狗的位置

he was not going to settle for anything less than being the leader.

他不会满足于成为领导者以外的任何角色。

Perrault took a hand in the chase to help catch the rebellious Buck.

佩罗参与了追捕，帮助抓住了叛逆的巴克。

Together, they ran him around the camp for nearly an hour.

他们一起带着他在营地里跑了将近一个小时。

They hurled clubs at him, but Buck dodged each one skillfully.

他们向他扔棍棒，但巴克巧妙地躲开了每一个棍棒。

They cursed him, his ancestors, his descendants, and every hair on him.

他们咒骂他、咒骂他的祖先、咒骂他的后代、咒骂他身上的每一根头发。

But Buck only snarled back and stayed just out of their reach.

但巴克只是咆哮着回应，并待在他们够不着的地方。

He never tried to run away but circled the camp deliberately.

他从未试图逃跑，而是故意绕着营地转。

He made it clear he was going to obey once they gave him what he wanted.

他明确表示，一旦他们满足了他的要求，他就会服从。

François finally sat down and scratched his head in frustration.

弗朗索瓦终于坐下来，沮丧地挠了挠头。

Perrault checked his watch, swore, and muttered about lost time.

佩罗看了看手表，咒骂着，嘟囔着浪费了时间。

An hour had already passed when they should have been on the trail.

本来应该上路的他们，现在已经过去了一个小时了。

François shrugged sheepishly at the courier, who sighed in defeat.

弗朗索瓦不好意思地对信使耸了耸肩，信使无奈地叹了口气。

Then François walked to Solleks and called out to Buck once more.

然后弗朗索瓦走到索莱克斯身边，再次呼唤巴克。

Buck laughed like a dog laughs, but kept his cautious distance.

巴克像狗一样笑，但仍然保持着谨慎的距离。

François removed Solleks's harness and returned him to his spot.

弗朗索瓦解下了索莱克斯的安全带，并将他放回原位。

The sled team stood fully harnessed, with only one spot unfilled.

雪橇队已全部装备完毕，只有一个位置空着。

The lead position remained empty, clearly meant for Buck alone.

领先位置仍然空着，显然是留给巴克一个人的。

François called again, and again Buck laughed and held his ground.

弗朗索瓦再次叫道，巴克再次大笑并坚守阵地。

"Throw down the club," Perrault ordered without hesitation.

"把棍棒扔下去。"佩罗毫不犹豫地命令道。

François obeyed, and Buck immediately trotted forward proudly.

弗朗索瓦服从了，巴克立即骄傲地向前小跑。

He laughed triumphantly and stepped into the lead position.

他得意地大笑起来，走上领头的位置。

François secured his traces, and the sled was broken loose.

弗朗索瓦固定住了牵引绳，雪橇松开了。

Both men ran alongside as the team raced onto the river trail.

当队伍冲向河边小道时，两人都并肩奔跑。

François had thought highly of Buck's "two devils,"

弗朗索瓦对巴克的"两个魔鬼"评价很高，

but he soon realized he had actually underestimated the dog.

但他很快意识到自己其实低估了这只狗。

Buck quickly assumed leadership and performed with excellence.

巴克很快就承担起了领导责任，并表现出色。

In judgment, quick thinking, and fast action, Buck surpassed Spitz.

在判断力、敏捷思维和快速行动方面，巴克超越了斯皮茨。

François had never seen a dog equal to what Buck now displayed.

弗朗索瓦从来没有见过一只狗能像巴克现在表现的那样。

But Buck truly excelled in enforcing order and commanding respect.

但巴克在维持秩序和赢得尊重方面确实表现出色。

Dave and Solleks accepted the change without concern or protest.

戴夫和索莱克斯毫无顾虑或抗议地接受了这一改变。

They focused only on work and pulling hard in the reins.

他们只专注于工作并全力以赴。

They cared little who led, so long as the sled kept moving.

他们并不关心谁领先，只要雪橇能够继续前进就行。

Billee, the cheerful one, could have led for all they cared.

比莉，性格开朗，本来可以担任领导，至于他们关心的是什么，那就由她来吧。

What mattered to them was peace and order in the ranks.
对他们来说，重要的是军队的和平与秩序。

The rest of the team had grown unruly during Spitz's decline.
在斯皮茨状态下滑期间，球队的其他成员也变得难以管教。

They were shocked when Buck immediately brought them to order.
当巴克立即让他们安静下来时，他们震惊了。

Pike had always been lazy and dragging his feet behind Buck.
派克总是很懒，总是跟在巴克后面。

But now was sharply disciplined by the new leadership.
但现在却受到了新领导层的严厉惩戒。

And he quickly learned to pull his weight in the team.
他很快就学会了在团队中发挥自己的作用。

By the end of the day, Pike worked harder than ever before.
到了这一天结束时，派克比以前更加努力地工作。

That night in camp, Joe, the sour dog, was finally subdued.
那天晚上在营地里，乔这只脾气暴躁的狗终于被制服了。

Spitz had failed to discipline him, but Buck did not fail.
斯皮茨未能管教好也，但巴克并没有失败。

Using his greater weight, Buck overwhelmed Joe in seconds.
巴克利用自己更强大的体重，在几秒钟内就制服了乔。

He bit and battered Joe until he whimpered and ceased resisting.
他不断咬乔，殴打他，直到乔呜咽一声并停止反抗。

The whole team improved from that moment on.
从那一刻起，整个团队都进步了。

The dogs regained their old unity and discipline.
狗又恢复了往日的团结和纪律。
At Rink Rapids, two new native huskies, Teek and Koona, joined.
在 Rink Rapids，两只新的本地哈士奇犬 Teek 和 Koona 加入了我们。
Buck's swift training of them astonished even François.
巴克对它们的快速训练甚至让弗朗索瓦感到惊讶。
"Never was there such a dog as that Buck!" he cried in amazement.
"从来没有过像巴克这样的狗！"他惊讶地喊道。
"No, never! He's worth one thousand dollars, by God!"
"不，绝对不！他值一千美元，我的天哪！"
"Eh? What do you say, Perrault?" he asked with pride.
"嗯？你说什么，佩罗？"他骄傲地问道。
Perrault nodded in agreement and checked his notes.
佩罗点头表示同意，并查看了他的笔记。
We're already ahead of schedule and gaining more each day.
我们已经提前完成了计划，并且每天都有收获。
The trail was hard-packed and smooth, with no fresh snow.
小路坚硬而平坦，没有新雪。
The cold was steady, hovering at fifty below zero throughout.
天气持续寒冷，气温始终徘徊在零下五十度左右。
The men rode and ran in turns to keep warm and make time.
男人们轮流骑马和跑步以保持温暖并节省时间。
The dogs ran fast with few stops, always pushing forward.
狗跑得很快，很少停下来，一直向前跑。
The Thirty Mile River was mostly frozen and easy to travel across.
三十英里河大部分已结冰，通行十分方便。
They went out in one day what had taken ten days coming in.
他们用一天的时间就完成了十天前才完成的工作。

They made a sixty-mile dash from Lake Le Barge to White Horse.
他们从勒巴日湖（Lake Le Barge）出发，奔跑了 60 英里到达白马湖（White Horse）。

Across Marsh, Tagish, and Bennett Lakes they moved incredibly fast.
它们以惊人的速度穿越马什湖、塔吉什湖和贝内特湖。

The running man towed behind the sled on a rope.
奔跑的人被一根绳子拖在雪橇后面。

On the last night of week two they got to their destination.
第二周的最后一晚，他们到达了目的地。

They had reached the top of White Pass together.
他们一起到达了白山口的顶峰。

They dropped down to sea level with Skaguay's lights below them.
他们下降到海平面，斯卡圭的灯光在他们下方。

It had been a record-setting run across miles of cold wilderness.
这是一次穿越数英里寒冷荒野的创纪录的奔跑。

For fourteen days straight, they averaged a strong forty miles.
连续十四天，他们平均行走四十英里。

In Skaguay, Perrault and François moved cargo through town.
在斯卡圭，佩罗和弗朗索瓦将货物运送到镇上。

They were cheered and offered many drinks by admiring crowds.
崇拜的人群为他们欢呼，并为他们提供了很多饮料。

Dog-busters and workers gathered around the famous dog team.
缉毒人员和工作人员聚集在这支著名的狗队周围。

Then western outlaws came to town and met violent defeat.
随后西方歹徒来到该镇并遭到惨败。

The people soon forgot the team and focused on new drama.

人们很快就忘记了这支球队，而把注意力集中在新的
戏剧上。

Then came the new orders that changed everything at once.
随后，新的命令下达，一切都立刻发生了改变。

François called Buck to him and hugged him with tearful pride.
弗朗索瓦把巴克叫到身边，满含泪水，自豪地拥抱了
他。

That moment was the last time Buck ever saw François again.
那一刻是巴克最后一次见到弗朗索瓦。

Like many men before, both François and Perrault were gone.
和之前的许多人一样，弗朗索瓦和佩罗都去世了。

A Scotch half-breed took charge of Buck and his sled dog teammates.
一名苏格兰混血儿负责照顾巴克和他的雪橇犬队友。

With a dozen other dog teams, they returned along the trail to Dawson.
他们与其他十几支狗队一起沿着小路返回道森。

It was no fast run now—just heavy toil with a heavy load each day.
现在不再是快速奔跑，而是每天辛苦劳作、负重前行
。

This was the mail train, bringing word to gold hunters near the Pole.
这是邮政列车，为北极附近的淘金者带来消息。

Buck disliked the work but bore it well, taking pride in his effort.
巴克不喜欢这项工作，但他很好地忍受了下来，并为
他的努力感到自豪。

Like Dave and Solleks, Buck showed devotion to every daily task.

和戴夫和索莱克斯一样，巴克对每一项日常任务都表现出极大的热情。

He made sure his teammates each pulled their fair weight.

他确保每个队友都尽到自己的责任。

Trail life became dull, repeated with the precision of a machine.

小径生活变得枯燥乏味，像机器一样精确地重复着。

Each day felt the same, one morning blending into the next.

每天的感觉都一样，一个早晨与下一个早晨融为一体。

At the same hour, the cooks rose to build fires and prepare food.

同一时间，厨师们起床生火准备食物。

After breakfast, some left camp while others harnessed the dogs.

早餐后，一些人离开营地，另一些人给狗牵上挽具。

They hit the trail before the dim warning of dawn touched the sky.

在黎明的微弱曙光尚未出现之前，他们就踏上了旅程。

At night, they stopped to make camp, each man with a set duty.

入夜后，他们停下来扎营，每个人都肩负着固定的职责。

Some pitched the tents, others cut firewood and gathered pine boughs.

一些人搭起帐篷，其他人砍柴并收集松枝。

Water or ice was carried back to the cooks for the evening meal.

水或冰被带回给厨师，供他们做晚餐。

The dogs were fed, and this was the best part of the day for them.

狗狗们吃饱了，这是它们一天中最美好的时光。

After eating fish, the dogs relaxed and lounged near the fire.

吃完鱼后，狗狗们就在火堆旁放松休息。

There were a hundred other dogs in the convoy to mingle with.

车队中还有一百只狗可以混在一起。

Many of those dogs were fierce and quick to fight without warning.

许多狗都很凶猛，而且会毫无预警地打架。

But after three wins, Buck mastered even the fiercest fighters.

但在三次胜利之后，巴克甚至战胜了最凶猛的战士。

Now when Buck growled and showed his teeth, they stepped aside.

现在，当巴克咆哮并露出牙齿时，他们就闪到一边。

Perhaps best of all, Buck loved lying near the flickering campfire.

也许最重要的是，巴克喜欢躺在摇曳的篝火旁。

He crouched with hind legs tucked and front legs stretched ahead.

他蹲下，后腿蜷缩，前腿向前伸直。

His head was raised as he blinked softly at the glowing flames.

他抬起头，对着炽热的火焰轻轻眨了眨眼。

Sometimes he recalled Judge Miller's big house in Santa Clara.

有时他会回忆起米勒法官在圣克拉拉的大房子。

He thought of the cement pool, of Ysabel, and the pug called Toots.

他想起了水泥池、伊莎贝尔和那只名叫图茨的哈巴狗。

But more often he remembered the man with the red sweater's club.

但他更多时候想起的是那个穿红毛衣的男人的棍棒。

He remembered Curly's death and his fierce battle with Spitz.

他记得卷毛的死，以及他与斯皮茨的激烈战斗。

He also recalled the good food he had eaten or still dreamed of.

他还回忆起曾经吃过或至今仍梦想着的美食。

Buck was not homesick—the warm valley was distant and unreal.

巴克并不想家——温暖的山谷遥远而不真实。

Memories of California no longer held any real pull over him.

加利福尼亚的记忆对他不再有任何真正的吸引力。

Stronger than memory were instincts deep in his bloodline.

比记忆更强大的是他血液深处的本能。

Habits once lost had returned, revived by the trail and the wild.

曾经失去的习惯又回来了，在小路和荒野中重新焕发活力。

As Buck watched the firelight, it sometimes became something else.

当巴克注视着火光时，它有时会变成别的东西。

He saw in the firelight another fire, older and deeper than the present one.

他在火光中看到了另一团火，比现在的火更古老、更深沉。

Beside that other fire crouched a man unlike the half-breed cook.

在那堆火旁边蹲着一个男人，与那个混血厨师不同。

This figure had short legs, long arms, and hard, knotted muscles.

这个人的腿很短，手臂很长，肌肉坚硬而紧绷。

His hair was long and matted, sloping backward from the eyes.

他的头发又长又乱，从眼睛处向后倾斜。

He made strange sounds and stared out in fear at the darkness.

他发出奇怪的声音并恐惧地盯着黑暗。

He held a stone club low, gripped tightly in his long rough hand.

他低手握着一根石棒，用他那只粗糙的长手紧紧地握着。

The man wore little; just a charred skin that hung down his back.

这个人穿得很少；只有一层烧焦的皮肤垂在背上。

His body was covered with thick hair across arms, chest, and thighs.

他的手臂、胸部和大腿上长满了浓密的毛发。

Some parts of the hair were tangled into patches of rough fur.

有些部分的毛发缠结成一片片粗糙的毛皮。

He did not stand straight but bent forward from the hips to knees.

他没有站直，而是从臀部到膝盖向前弯曲。

His steps were springy and catlike, as if always ready to leap.

他的步伐轻快，像猫一样，仿佛随时准备跳跃。

There was a sharp alertness, like he lived in constant fear.

他高度警惕，仿佛生活在持续的恐惧之中。

This ancient man seemed to expect danger, whether the danger was seen or not.

这位老人似乎预料到了危险，无论是否看到了危险。

At times the hairy man slept by the fire, head tucked between legs.

有时，这个毛茸茸的男人会睡在火堆旁，头埋在两腿之间。

His elbows rested on his knees, hands clasped above his head.

他的手肘放在膝盖上，双手交叉放在头顶。

Like a dog he used his hairy arms to shed off the falling rain.

他像狗一样用毛茸茸的手臂甩掉落下的雨水。

Beyond the firelight, Buck saw twin coals glowing in the dark.

在火光的远处，巴克看到两块煤在黑暗中闪闪发光。

Always two by two, they were the eyes of stalking beasts of prey.

它们总是成双成对，就像潜行的猛兽的眼睛。

He heard bodies crash through brush and sounds made in the night.

他听到了尸体撞破灌木丛的声音和夜晚发出的声音。

Lying on the Yukon bank, blinking, Buck dreamed by the fire.

巴克躺在育空河岸上，眨着眼睛，在火堆旁做着梦。

The sights and sounds of that wild world made his hair stand up.

那个狂野世界的景象和声音让他毛骨悚然。

The fur rose along his back, his shoulders, and up his neck.

毛发沿着他的背部、肩膀和脖子向上生长。

He whimpered softly or gave a low growl deep in his chest.

他轻轻地呜咽着，或者从胸腔深处发出低沉的咆哮声。

Then the half-breed cook shouted, "Hey, you Buck, wake up!"

这时，混血厨师喊道："嘿，巴克，你醒醒！"

The dream world vanished, and real life returned to Buck's eyes.

梦境消失了，现实生活又回到了巴克的眼前。

He was going to get up, stretch, and yawn, as if woken from a nap.

他要起身、伸伸懒腰、打个哈欠，就像刚从午睡中醒来一样。

The trip was hard, with the mail sled dragging behind them.

这次旅行非常艰难，因为后面拖着邮件雪橇。

Heavy loads and tough work wore down the dogs each long day.

每天漫长的时光里，沉重的负担和艰苦的工作让狗精疲力竭。

They reached Dawson thin, tired, and needing over a week's rest.

他们到达道森时已经又瘦又累，需要休息一个多星期。

But only two days later, they set out down the Yukon again.

但仅仅两天后，他们就再次踏上了育空河之旅。

They were loaded with more letters bound for the outside world.

船上装载着更多发往外界的信件。

The dogs were exhausted and the men were complaining constantly.

狗已经筋疲力尽，而男人们也不断抱怨。

Snow fell every day, softening the trail and slowing the sleds.

每天都会下雪，导致雪道变软，雪橇的速度变慢。

This made for harder pulling and more drag on the runners.

这使得拉动变得更加困难，并且对跑步者的阻力也更大。

Despite that, the drivers were fair and cared for their teams.

尽管如此，车手们还是很公平并且关心他们的车队。

Each night, the dogs were fed before the men got to eat.

每天晚上，狗都会在男人们吃饭之前先吃饱。

No man slept before checking the feet of his own dog's.

没有人会在睡觉前检查自己狗的脚。

Still, the dogs grew weaker as the miles wore on their bodies.

然而，随着长途跋涉，狗的身体变得越来越虚弱。

They had traveled eighteen hundred miles through the winter.

整个冬天他们已经旅行了一千八百英里。

They pulled sleds across every mile of that brutal distance.

他们拉着雪橇走过那段残酷的距离的每一英里。

Even the toughest sled dogs feel strain after so many miles.

即使是最强壮的雪橇犬，在跑了这么长的距离之后也会感到疲惫。

Buck held on, kept his team working, and maintained discipline.

巴克坚持了下来，让团队继续工作，并保持纪律。

But Buck was tired, just like the others on the long journey.

但是巴克很累，就像其他长途旅行的人一样。

Billee whimpered and cried in his sleep each night without fail.

比利每晚都会在睡梦中呜咽哭泣。

Joe grew even more bitter, and Solleks stayed cold and distant.

乔变得更加痛苦，而索莱克斯则变得冷漠而疏远。

But it was Dave who suffered the worst out of the entire team.

但在整个团队中，戴夫的受害最为严重。

Something had gone wrong inside him, though no one knew what.

他内心出了问题，但没人知道是什么。

He became moodier and snapped at others with growing anger.

他变得越来越喜怒无常，并且越来越愤怒地对别人厉声斥责。

Each night he went straight to his nest, waiting to be fed.

每天晚上，他都会直接回到自己的巢穴，等待喂食。

Once he was down, Dave did not get up again till morning.

倒下之后，戴夫直到早上才再次起床。

On the reins, sudden jerks or starts made him cry out in pain.

缰绳突然猛地一拉或一震，就会让他痛得大叫。

His driver searched for the cause, but found no injury on him.

他的司机寻找事故原因，但未发现他受伤。

All the drivers began watching Dave and discussed his case.

所有司机都开始关注戴夫并讨论他的情况。

They talked at meals and during their final smoke of the day.
他们在吃饭时和一天中最后抽烟时聊天。

One night they held a meeting and brought Dave to the fire.
一天晚上，他们开了个会，并把戴夫带到了火堆旁。

They pressed and probed his body, and he cried out often.
他们按压、检查他的身体，他经常哭喊。

Clearly, something was wrong, though no bones seemed broken.
显然，有些地方出了问题，尽管骨头似乎没有断裂。

By the time they reached Cassiar Bar, Dave was falling down.
当他们到达卡西亚酒吧时，戴夫已经倒下了。

The Scotch half-breed called a halt and removed Dave from the team.
这位苏格兰混血儿叫停了比赛，并将戴夫从球队中除名。

He fastened Solleks in Dave's place, closest to the sled's front.
他把索莱克斯固定在戴夫的位置上，靠近雪橇的前部。

He meant to let Dave rest and run free behind the moving sled.
他想让戴夫休息并在移动的雪橇后面自由奔跑。

But even sick, Dave hated being taken from the job he had owned.
但即使生病了，戴夫仍然讨厌被剥夺他原来的工作。

He growled and whimpered as the reins were pulled from his body.
当缰绳从他的身体上被拔出时，他发出咆哮和呜咽声。

When he saw Solleks in his place, he cried with broken-hearted pain.
当他看到索莱克斯站在自己的位置上时，他伤心欲绝，哭了起来。

The pride of trail work was deep in Dave, even as death approached.

即使死亡临近，戴夫心中仍然怀有从事越野跑工作的深深自豪感。

As the sled moved, Dave floundered through soft snow near the trail.

随着雪橇的移动，戴夫在小路附近的松软雪地上挣扎。

He attacked Solleks, biting and pushing him from the sled's side.

他攻击了索莱克斯，咬了他并将他从雪橇侧面推开。

Dave tried to leap into the harness and reclaim his working spot.

戴夫试图跳进安全带并重新夺回他的工作位置。

He yelped, whined, and cried, torn between pain and pride in labor.

他尖叫、呜咽、哭泣，在分娩的痛苦和自豪之间挣扎。

The half-breed used his whip to try driving Dave away from the team.

这个混血儿用鞭子试图把戴夫赶出队伍。

But Dave ignored the lash, and the man couldn't strike him harder.

但戴夫无视了鞭子，那人无法更用力地打他。

Dave refused the easier path behind the sled, where snow was packed.

戴夫拒绝选择雪橇后面更容易走的路，因为那里积满了雪。

Instead, he struggled in the deep snow beside the trail, in misery.

相反，他在小路旁的深雪中痛苦地挣扎。

Eventually, Dave collapsed, lying in the snow and howling in pain.

最终，戴夫倒下了，躺在雪地里痛苦地嚎叫。

He cried out as the long train of sleds passed him one by one.

当长长的雪橇队伍一辆接一辆地从他身边驶过时，他大声喊道。

Still, with what strength remained, he rose and stumbled after them.

尽管如此，他还是凭借着仅存的力气站了起来，跌跌撞撞地跟在他们后面。

He caught up when the train stopped again and found his old sled.

当火车再次停下来时，他追了上来，找到了他的旧雪橇。

He floundered past the other teams and stood beside Solleks again.

他奋力超越其他队伍，再次站在索莱克斯身边。

As the driver paused to light his pipe, Dave took his last chance.

当司机停下来点燃烟斗时，戴夫抓住了最后的机会。

When the driver returned and shouted, the team didn't move forward.

当司机返回并大喊时，车队没有继续前进。

The dogs had turned their heads, confused by the sudden stoppage.

狗儿们因为突然的停顿而感到困惑，纷纷转过头。

The driver was shocked too—the sled hadn't moved an inch forward.

驾驶员也大吃一惊——
雪橇根本就没向前移动一英寸。

He called out to the others to come and see what had happened.

他大声呼喊其他人过来看看发生了什么事。

Dave had chewed through Solleks's reins, breaking both apart.

戴夫咬断了索莱克斯的缰绳，把两者都咬断了。

Now he stood in front of the sled, back in his rightful
position.

现在他站在雪橇前面，回到了他正确的位置。

Dave looked up at the driver, silently pleading to stay in the
traces.

戴夫抬头看着司机，默默地恳求他留在车道上。

The driver was puzzled, unsure of what to do for the
struggling dog.

司机感到困惑，不知道该如何帮助这只挣扎的狗。

The other men spoke of dogs who had died from being
taken out.

其他人谈到了因被带出去而死亡的狗。

They told of old or injured dogs whose hearts broke when
left behind.

他们讲述了那些年老或受伤的狗被遗弃时心碎的故事
。

They agreed it was mercy to let Dave die while still in his
harness.

他们一致认为，让戴夫在安全带里死去是仁慈的。

He was fastened back onto the sled, and Dave pulled with
pride.

他被重新绑在雪橇上，戴夫自豪地拉着雪橇。

Though he cried out at times, he worked as if pain could be
ignored.

尽管他有时会大叫，但他仍然努力工作，仿佛可以忽
略痛苦。

More than once he fell and was dragged before rising again.

他不止一次跌倒，被人拖着才再次站起来。

Once, the sled rolled over him, and he limped from that
moment on.

有一次，雪橇从他身上滚了过去，从那一刻起他就一
瘸一拐地走路了。

Still, he worked until camp was reached, and then lay by the
fire.

尽管如此，他还是坚持工作直到到达营地，然后躺在火堆旁。

By morning, Dave was too weak to travel or even stand upright.

到了早上，戴夫已经虚弱得无法行走，甚至无法站立。

At harness-up time, he tried to reach his driver with trembling effort.

在系好马具时，他颤抖着努力试图靠近他的车夫。

He forced himself up, staggered, and collapsed onto the snowy ground.

他强迫自己站起来，却踉跄了一下，倒在了雪地上。

Using his front legs, he dragged his body toward the harnessing area.

他用前腿将身体拖向挽具区域。

He hitched himself forward, inch by inch, toward the working dogs.

他一点一点地向前移动，向工作犬靠近。

His strength gave out, but he kept moving in his last desperate push.

他已经筋疲力尽，但他仍在拼尽最后一丝力气，继续前行。

His teammates saw him gasping in the snow, still longing to join them.

队友们看到他在雪地里喘着粗气，仍然渴望加入他们。

They heard him howling with sorrow as they left the camp behind.

当他们离开营地时，听到了他悲伤的嚎叫。

As the team vanished into trees, Dave's cry echoed behind them.

当队伍消失在树林中时，戴夫的叫喊声在他们身后回荡。

The sled train halted briefly after crossing a stretch of river timber.

雪橇火车穿过一片河边树林后短暂地停了下来。

The Scotch half-breed walked slowly back toward the camp behind.

苏格兰混血儿慢慢地向后面的营地走去。

The men stopped speaking when they saw him leave the sled train.

当人们看到他离开雪橇列车时，他们停止了说话。

Then a single gunshot rang out clear and sharp across the trail.

然后，小路上响起了一声清晰而尖锐的枪声。

The man returned quickly and took up his place without a word.

那人很快就回来了，一言不发地回到了自己的位置。

Whips cracked, bells jingled, and the sleds rolled on through snow.

鞭子啪啪作响，铃铛叮当作响，雪橇在雪地里滚动。

But Buck knew what had happened—and so did every other dog.

但巴克知道发生了什么事——其他狗也知道。

The Toil of Reins and Trail
缰绳与踪迹的辛劳

Thirty days after leaving Dawson, the Salt Water Mail reached Skaguay.
离开道森三十天后，咸水邮船抵达斯卡圭。

Buck and his teammates pulled the lead, arriving in pitiful condition.
巴克和他的队友们领先，但到达时他们的状态却很糟糕。

Buck had dropped from one hundred forty to one hundred fifteen pounds.
巴克的体重从一百四十磅减到了一百一十五磅。

The other dogs, though smaller, had lost even more body weight.
其他狗虽然体型较小，但体重减轻得更多。

Pike, once a fake limper, now dragged a truly injured leg behind him.
派克曾经假装跛脚，现在却拖着一条真正受伤的腿。

Solleks was limping badly, and Dub had a wrenched shoulder blade.
索莱克斯（Solleks）严重跛行，而杜布（Dub）的肩胛骨则扭伤了。

Every dog in the team was footsore from weeks on the frozen trail.
由于在冰冻的小路上跋涉了数周，队伍中的每只狗都脚痛不已。

They had no spring left in their steps, only slow, dragging motion.
他们的步伐不再轻快，只有缓慢、拖沓的动作。

Their feet hit the trail hard, each step adding more strain to their bodies.
他们的双脚用力踩在小路上，每一步都给他们的身体带来更大的压力。

They were not sick, only drained beyond all natural recovery.

他们并没有生病，只是体力消耗太大，无法自然恢复。

This was not tiredness from one hard day, cured with a night's rest.

这不是一天辛苦劳累之后，经过一夜休息就能治愈的疲劳。

It was exhaustion built slowly through months of grueling effort.

这是经过数月艰苦努力慢慢积累起来的疲惫。

No reserve strength remained—they had used up every bit they had.

没有任何后备力量，他们已经用尽了所有的力量。

Every muscle, fiber, and cell in their bodies was spent and worn.

他们身上的每一块肌肉、每一根纤维、每一个细胞都已磨损殆尽。

And there was a reason—they had covered twenty-five hundred miles.

这是有原因的——他们已经走了两千五百英里。

They had rested only five days during the last eighteen hundred miles.

在最后的一千八百英里中，他们只休息了五天。

When they reached Skaguay, they looked barely able to stand upright.

当他们到达斯卡圭时，他们看起来几乎无法直立。

They struggled to keep the reins tight and stay ahead of the sled.

他们努力拉紧缰绳·保持领先于雪橇。

On downhill slopes, they only managed to avoid being run over.

在下坡时，他们仅仅设法避免被碾压。

"March on, poor sore feet," the driver said as they limped along.

"继续前进吧，可怜的脚，好痛啊，"司机一边说着，一边一瘸一拐地往前走。

"This is the last stretch, then we all get one long rest, for sure."

"这是最后一段路程，然后我们肯定都会得到一次长时间的休息。"

"One truly long rest," he promised, watching them stagger forward.

"一次真正长久的休息，"他承诺道，看着他们蹒跚地向前走。

The drivers expected they were going to now get a long, needed break.

司机们希望他们现在可以得到一次长时间的、必要的休息。

They had traveled twelve hundred miles with only two days' rest.

他们已经走了一千二百英里，只休息了两天。

By fairness and reason, they felt they had earned time to relax.

公平而理性地，他们觉得自己应该有时间放松一下。

But too many had come to the Klondike, and too few had stayed home.

但是来到克朗代克的人太多了，而留在家里的人太少了。

Letters from families flooded in, creating piles of delayed mail.

来自家人的信件大量涌入，导致大量邮件被延误。

Official orders arrived—new Hudson Bay dogs were going to take over.

官方命令已下达——新的哈德逊湾犬将接管。

The exhausted dogs, now called worthless, were to be disposed of.

这些筋疲力尽的狗现在被认为毫无价值，将被处理掉。

Since money mattered more than dogs, they were going to
be sold cheaply.
因为钱比狗更重要，所以它们将被廉价出售。
Three more days passed before the dogs felt just how weak
they were.
又过了三天，狗才感觉到自己有多么虚弱。
On the fourth morning, two men from the States bought the
whole team.
第四天早上，两个来自美国的男人买下了整支球队。
The sale included all the dogs, plus their worn harness gear.
此次出售的商品包括所有狗以及它们磨损的挽具。
The men called each other "Hal" and "Charles" as they
completed the deal.
交易完成后，两人互称"哈尔"和"查尔斯"。
Charles was middle-aged, pale, with limp lips and fierce
mustache tips.
查尔斯是一位中年人，面色苍白，嘴唇松弛，胡子尖
儿浓密。
Hal was a young man, maybe nineteen, wearing a cartridge-
stuffed belt.
哈尔是个年轻人，大概十九岁，腰间系着一条装满子
弹的腰带。
The belt held a big revolver and a hunting knife, both
unused.
腰带上挂着一把大左轮手枪和一把猎刀，均未使用过
。
It showed how inexperienced and unfit he was for northern
life.
这表明他缺乏经验，不适合北方的生活。
Neither man belonged in the wild; their presence defied all
reason.
这两个人都不属于荒野；他们的存在违背了一切理性
。
Buck watched as money exchanged hands between buyer
and agent.

巴克看着买家和代理人之间金钱交易。

He knew the mail-train drivers were leaving his life like the rest.

他知道，邮政火车司机也像其他人一样，要离开他的生活了。

They followed Perrault and François, now gone beyond recall.

他们追随了佩罗和弗朗索瓦的脚步，而后者如今已不在人世。

Buck and the team were led to their new owners' sloppy camp.

巴克和球队被带到了新主人的简陋营地。

The tent sagged, dishes were dirty, and everything lay in disarray.

帐篷塌陷，盘子脏兮兮的，一切都乱七八糟。

Buck noticed a woman there too—Mercedes, Charles's wife and Hal's sister.

巴克也注意到那里有一个女人——
梅赛德斯，查尔斯的妻子，哈尔的妹妹。

They made a complete family, though far from suited to the trail.

尽管他们远不适合这条路线，但他们组成了一个完整的家庭。

Buck watched nervously as the trio started packing the supplies.

巴克紧张地看着三人开始打包物资。

They worked hard but without order—just fuss and wasted effort.

他们努力工作，但没有秩序——
只是忙乱和浪费精力。

The tent was rolled into a bulky shape, far too large for the sled.

帐篷被卷成一个笨重的形状，对于雪橇来说太大了。

Dirty dishes were packed without being cleaned or dried at all.

脏盘子根本没有清洗或擦干就被打包了。

Mercedes fluttered about, constantly talking, correcting, and meddling.

梅赛德斯四处飞舞，不断地说话、纠正和干涉。

When a sack was placed on front, she insisted it go on the back.

当一个袋子放在前面时，她坚持把它放在后面。

She packed the sack in the bottom, and the next moment she needed it.

她把麻袋塞在底部，下一刻她就需要它了。

So the sled was unpacked again to reach the one specific bag.

因此，雪橇再次被打开，以到达一个特定的袋子。

Nearby, three men stood outside a tent, watching the scene unfold.

附近，三名男子站在帐篷外，注视着这一幕的发生。

They smiled, winked, and grinned at the newcomers' obvious confusion.

他们微笑着，眨眨眼，对新来者明显困惑的表情咧嘴一笑。

"You've got a right heavy load already," said one of the men.

"你已经扛了很重的担子了，"其中一名男子说道。

"I don't think you should carry that tent, but it's your choice."

"我认为你不应该扛着那顶帐篷，但这是你的选择。"

"Undreamed of!" cried Mercedes, throwing up her hands in despair.

"做梦也想不到！"梅赛德斯绝望地举起双手，大叫道。

"How could I possibly travel without a tent to stay under?"

"没有帐篷我怎么能去旅行呢？"

"It's springtime—you won't see cold weather again," the man replied.

"现在是春天——
你不会再看到寒冷的天气了，"那人回答道。

But she shook her head, and they kept piling items onto the sled.

但她摇了摇头，他们继续把物品堆到雪橇上。

The load towered dangerously high as they added the final things.

当他们添加最后的东西时，负载已经高得危险了。

"Think the sled will ride?" asked one of the men with a skeptical look.

"你觉得雪橇能滑行吗？"其中一个男人怀疑地问道。

"Why shouldn't it?" Charles snapped back with sharp annoyance.

"为什么不能呢？"查尔斯恼怒地反驳道。

"Oh, that's all right," the man said quickly, backing away from offense.

"哦，没关系，"那人赶紧说道，不再冒犯。

"I was only wondering—it just looked a bit too top-heavy to me."

"我只是好奇——
它看起来对我来说有点头重脚轻。"

Charles turned away and tied down the load as best as he could.

查尔斯转过身，尽力把货物绑好。

But the lashings were loose and the packing poorly done overall.

但捆扎松散，整体包装质量较差。

"Sure, the dogs will pull that all day," another man said sarcastically.

"当然，狗会整天拉这个，"另一个男人讽刺地说。

"Of course," Hal replied coldly, grabbing the sled's long gee-pole.

"当然，"哈尔冷冷地回答道，抓住了雪橇的长地杆。

With one hand on the pole, he swung the whip in the other.

他一手扶着杆子，一手挥动着鞭子。

"Let's go!" he shouted. "Move it!" urging the dogs to start.

"出发！"他喊道。"动起来！"他催促着狗们开始行动。

The dogs leaned into the harness and strained for a few moments.

狗靠在挽具上，用力了一会儿。

Then they stopped, unable to budge the overloaded sled an inch.

然后他们停了下来，超载的雪橇一动也不能动。

"The lazy brutes!" Hal yelled, lifting the whip to strike them.

"这些懒惰的畜生！"哈尔喊道，举起鞭子抽打他们。

But Mercedes rushed in and seized the whip from Hal's hands.

但梅赛德斯冲了进来，从哈尔手中夺走了鞭子。

"Oh, Hal, don't you dare hurt them," she cried in alarm.

"哦，哈尔，你敢伤害他们，"她惊慌地喊道。

"Promise me you'll be kind to them, or I won't go another step."

"答应我，你会善待他们，否则我就不再前进一步。"

"You don't know a thing about dogs," Hal snapped at his sister.

"你对狗一无所知"哈尔厉声对妹妹说。

"They're lazy, and the only way to move them is to whip them."

"他们很懒，唯一能让他们动起来的方法就是鞭打他们。"

"Ask anyone—ask one of those men over there if you doubt me."

"如果你怀疑我，就问任何人——
问那边的那些人中的一个。"

Mercedes looked at the onlookers with pleading, tearful eyes.

梅赛德斯用恳求和泪眼看着旁观者。

Her face showed how deeply she hated the sight of any pain.

她的脸上流露出她对看到任何痛苦的极度厌恶。

"They're weak, that's all," one man said. "They're worn out."

"他们只是虚弱而已，"一名男子说道，"他们已经筋疲力尽了。"

"They need rest—they've been worked too long without a break."

"他们需要休息——
他们已经工作太久了，没有休息过。"

"Rest be cursed," Hal muttered with his lip curled.

"剩下的就见鬼去吧，"哈尔撇着嘴嘟囔道。

Mercedes gasped, clearly pained by the coarse word from him.

梅赛德斯倒吸了一口气，显然被他粗鲁的言辞弄得很痛苦。

Still, she stayed loyal and instantly defended her brother.

尽管如此，她仍然保持忠诚并立即保护了她的兄弟。

"Don't mind that man," she said to Hal. "They're our dogs."

"别介意那个男人，"她对哈尔说。"它们是我们的狗。"

"You drive them as you see fit—do what you think is right."

"你按照自己认为合适的方式驾驶它们——
做你认为正确的事。"

Hal raised the whip and struck the dogs again without mercy.

哈尔举起鞭子，再次毫不留情地抽打狗。

They lunged forward, bodies low, feet pushing into the snow.

他们猛地向前冲去，身体放低，双脚深深地插入雪中
。

All their strength went into the pull, but the sled wasn't
moving.
他们用尽全身的力气去拉，但雪橇却纹丝不动。

The sled stayed stuck, like an anchor frozen into the packed
snow.
雪橇卡住了，就像一个锚被冻在了厚厚的雪里。

After a second effort, the dogs stopped again, panting hard.
经过第二次尝试，狗再次停了下来，气喘吁吁。

Hal raised the whip once more, just as Mercedes interfered
again.
就在梅赛德斯再次出手阻拦时，哈尔再次举起了鞭子
。

She dropped to her knees in front of Buck and hugged his
neck.
她跪在巴克面前并抱住他的脖子。

Tears filled her eyes as she pleaded with the exhausted dog.
当她恳求这只筋疲力尽的狗时，她的眼里充满了泪水
。

"You poor dears," she said, "why don't you just pull
harder?"
"你这可怜的孩子，" 她说，"为什么不再用力拉一
点呢？"

"If you pull, then you won't get to be whipped like this."
"如果你拉的话，就不会被这样鞭打了。"

Buck disliked Mercedes, but he was too tired to resist her
now.
巴克不喜欢梅赛德斯，但是他现在太累了，无法抗拒
她。

He accepted her tears as just another part of the miserable
day.
他把她的眼泪当做这悲惨的一天的一部分。

One of the watching men finally spoke after holding back his anger.

一名围观的男子终于强忍住怒火，开口说道。

"I don't care what happens to you folks, but those dogs matter."

"我不关心你们发生了什么，但那些狗很重要。"

"If you want to help, break that sled loose—it's frozen to the snow."

"如果你想帮忙，就把雪橇松开——
它已经冻在雪上了。"

"Push hard on the gee-pole, right and left, and break the ice seal."

"用力推航向杆，左右推动，打破冰封。"

A third attempt was made, this time following the man's suggestion.

第三次尝试之后，这次听从了该男子的建议。

Hal rocked the sled from side to side, breaking the runners loose.

哈尔左右摇晃着雪橇，把滑板摇松了。

The sled, though overloaded and awkward, finally lurched forward.

雪橇虽然超载且笨重，但最终还是向前蹒跚而行。

Buck and the others pulled wildly, driven by a storm of whiplashes.

巴克和其他人疯狂地拉着船，被一阵鞭子抽打着。

A hundred yards ahead, the trail curved and sloped into the street.

前方一百码处，小路弯曲并倾斜进入街道。

It was going to have taken a skilled driver to keep the sled upright.

需要一位熟练的驾驶员才能保持雪橇直立。

Hal was not skilled, and the sled tipped as it swung around the bend.

哈尔的技术并不熟练，雪橇在转弯时倾斜了。

Loose lashings gave way, and half the load spilled onto the snow.

松散的捆扎带断裂，一半的货物散落在雪地上。

The dogs did not stop; the lighter sled flew along on its side.

狗没有停下来；较轻的雪橇侧身飞驰而去。

Angry from abuse and the heavy burden, the dogs ran faster.

由于受到虐待和负担过重，狗变得愤怒，跑得更快了。

Buck, in fury, broke into a run, with the team following behind.

巴克勃然大怒，拔腿就跑，队伍紧随其后。

Hal shouted "Whoa! Whoa!" but the team paid no attention to him.

哈尔大喊"哇！哇！"但队员们没有理会他。

He tripped, fell, and was dragged along the ground by the harness.

他绊倒了，摔倒了，被安全带拖着在地上行走。

The overturned sled bumped over him as the dogs raced on ahead.

当狗在前面奔跑时，翻倒的雪橇撞到了他。

The rest of the supplies scattered across Skaguay's busy street.

其余物资散落在斯卡圭繁忙的街道上。

Kind-hearted people rushed to stop the dogs and gather the gear.

好心人赶紧上前阻止，并收拾好装备。

They also gave advice, blunt and practical, to the new travelers.

他们还向新旅行者提供了直率而实用的建议。

"If you want to reach Dawson, take half the load and double the dogs."

"如果你想到达道森，就带一半的货物，双倍的狗。"

Hal, Charles, and Mercedes listened, though not with enthusiasm.

哈尔、查尔斯和梅赛德斯听着，但并不热情。

They pitched their tent and started sorting through their supplies.

他们搭起帐篷并开始整理物资。

Out came canned goods, which made onlookers laugh aloud.

罐头食品端了出来，引得围观的人哈哈大笑。

"Canned stuff on the trail? You'll starve before that melts," one said.

"路上有罐头食品？等它们融化了你就会饿死的。"一个人说道。

"Hotel blankets? You're better off throwing them all out."

"酒店的毯子？你最好把它们都扔掉。"

"Ditch the tent, too, and no one washes dishes here."

"把帐篷也扔掉，这里就没人洗碗了。"

"You think you're riding a Pullman train with servants on board?"

"你以为你乘坐的是一辆有仆人的普尔曼火车吗？"

The process began—every useless item was tossed to the side.

流程开始了——所有无用的物品都被扔到一边。

Mercedes cried when her bags were emptied onto the snowy ground.

当她的行李被倒在雪地上时，梅赛德斯哭了。

She sobbed over every item thrown out, one by one without pause.

她对着被扔掉的每件物品不停地抽泣。

She vowed not to go one more step—not even for ten Charleses.

她发誓不再向前迈进一步——哪怕是十个查尔斯。

She begged each person nearby to let her keep her precious things.

她恳求附近的每个人让她保留她的珍贵物品。

At last, she wiped her eyes and began tossing even vital clothes.

最后，她擦干了眼睛，开始扔掉哪怕是至关重要的衣
服。

When done with her own, she began emptying the men's supplies.

当她处理完自己的物品后，她开始清空男人们的物品
。

Like a whirlwind, she tore through Charles and Hal's belongings.

她像旋风一样，把查尔斯和哈尔的物品都洗劫一空。

Though the load was halved, it was still far heavier than needed.

尽管负载减少了一半，但仍然远远超过了需要的重量
。

That night, Charles and Hal went out and bought six new dogs.

那天晚上，查尔斯和哈尔出去买了六只新狗。

These new dogs joined the original six, plus Teek and Koona.

这些新狗加入了原来的六只狗，还有 Teek 和
Koona。

Together they made a team of fourteen dogs hitched to the sled.

他们一起组成了一支由十四只狗组成的队伍，这些狗
都被拴在雪橇上。

But the new dogs were unfit and poorly trained for sled work.

但新来的狗不适合拉雪橇，训练也很差。

Three of the dogs were short-haired pointers, and one was a Newfoundland.

其中三只狗是短毛指示犬，一只是纽芬兰犬。

The final two dogs were mutts of no clear breed or purpose at all.

最后两只狗是杂种狗，没有明确的品种或用途。

They didn't understand the trail, and they didn't learn it quickly.

他们不了解这条路线，而且他们没有很快学会它。

Buck and his mates watched them with scorn and deep irritation.

巴克和他的伙伴们带着轻蔑和深深的恼怒看着他们。

Though Buck taught them what not to do, he could not teach duty.

尽管巴克教会了他们什么不该做，但他却无法教会他们责任。

They didn't take well to trail life or the pull of reins and sleds.

它们不适应跟踪生活，也不适应缰绳和雪橇的拉动。

Only the mongrels tried to adapt, and even they lacked fighting spirit.

只有杂种狗试图适应，但即使如此，它们也缺乏战斗精神。

The other dogs were confused, weakened, and broken by their new life.

其他狗对新生活感到困惑、虚弱和崩溃。

With the new dogs clueless and the old ones exhausted, hope was thin.

由于新来的狗毫无头绪，而老狗又筋疲力尽，希望渺茫。

Buck's team had covered twenty-five hundred miles of harsh trail.

巴克的队伍已经走过了二千五百英里的艰难道路。

Still, the two men were cheerful and proud of their large dog team.

尽管如此，这两个人还是很高兴，并为他们的大型狗队感到自豪。

They thought they were traveling in style, with fourteen dogs hitched.

他们以为带着十四只狗的旅行很时尚。

They had seen sleds leave for Dawson, and others arrive from it.

他们看到雪橇出发前往道森，其他雪橇也从那里抵达。

But never had they seen one pulled by as many as fourteen dogs.
但他们从未见过由十四只狗拉着的火车。

There was a reason such teams were rare in the Arctic wilderness.
这样的队伍在北极荒野中很少见，这是有原因的。

No sled could carry enough food to feed fourteen dogs for the trip.
没有一辆雪橇能够装载足够的食物来喂养十四只狗。

But Charles and Hal didn't know that—they had done the math.
但查尔斯和哈尔不知道这一点——他们已经算过了。

They penciled out the food: so much per dog, so many days, done.
他们用铅笔写下食物量：每只狗需要多少，需要多少天，就吃完。

Mercedes looked at their figures and nodded as if it made sense.
梅赛德斯看着他们的身影，点了点头，仿佛觉得很有道理。

It all seemed very simple to her, at least on paper.
对她来说，一切都显得非常简单，至少在纸面上是如此。

The next morning, Buck led the team slowly up the snowy street.
第二天早上，巴克带领队伍沿着积雪的街道缓缓前行。

There was no energy or spirit in him or the dogs behind him.
他和他身后的狗都失去了活力和精神。

They were dead tired from the start—there was no reserve left.

他们从一开始就非常疲惫——没有任何后劲。

Buck had made four trips between Salt Water and Dawson already.

巴克已在 Salt Water 和 Dawson 之间往返了四次。

Now, faced with the same trail again, he felt nothing but bitterness.

如今，再次面临同样的考验，他只感到苦涩。

His heart was not in it, nor were the hearts of the other dogs.

他心不在焉，其他狗也一样。

The new dogs were timid, and the huskies lacked all trust.

新来的狗很胆小，哈士奇也缺乏信任。

Buck sensed he could not rely on these two men or their sister.

巴克感觉到他不能依赖这两个人或他们的妹妹。

They knew nothing and showed no signs of learning on the trail.

他们什么都不知道，而且在路上也没有表现出任何学习的迹象。

They were disorganized and lacked any sense of discipline.

他们组织混乱，缺乏纪律性。

It took them half the night to set up a sloppy camp each time.

每次他们都要花半夜的时间才能搭建一个简陋的营地。

And half the next morning they spent fumbling with the sled again.

第二天上午他们又花了大半天时间笨手笨脚地推着雪橇。

By noon, they often stopped just to fix the uneven load.

到了中午，他们常常会停下来只是为了修理不均匀的负载。

On some days, they traveled less than ten miles in total.

有些日子，他们总共行走不到十英里。

Other days, they didn't manage to leave camp at all.

其他日子里，他们根本没能离开营地。

They never came close to covering the planned food-distance.

他们从来没有接近完成计划的食物距离。

As expected, they ran short on food for the dogs very quickly.

正如他们所料，狗粮很快就吃完了。

They made matters worse by overfeeding in the early days.

早期他们喂食过多，导致情况变得更糟。

This brought starvation closer with every careless ration.

每一次不注意配给，都使饥饿离我们越来越近。

The new dogs had not learned to survive on very little.

新来的狗还没有学会如何靠很少的资源生存。

They ate hungrily, with appetites too large for the trail.

他们狼吞虎咽地吃着东西，胃口太大，不适合走这条路。

Seeing the dogs weaken, Hal believed the food wasn't enough.

看到狗越来越虚弱，哈尔认为食物不够。

He doubled the rations, making the mistake even worse.

他把口粮增加了一倍，这使错误变得更加严重。

Mercedes added to the problem with tears and soft pleading.

梅赛德斯的眼泪和轻声的恳求让问题变得更加严重。

When she couldn't convince Hal, she fed the dogs in secret.

当她无法说服哈尔时，她就偷偷地喂狗。

She stole from the fish sacks and gave it to them behind his back.

她偷走了鱼袋里的鱼，并背着他给了他们。

But what the dogs truly needed wasn't more food—it was rest.

但狗真正需要的不是更多的食物，而是休息。

They were making poor time, but the heavy sled still dragged on.

他们的速度很慢，但沉重的雪橇仍然向前移动。

That weight alone drained their remaining strength each day.

单是这个重量就足以消耗他们每天仅剩的体力。

Then came the stage of underfeeding as the supplies ran low.

随后，由于供给不足，进入了食物不足的阶段。

Hal realized one morning that half the dog food was already gone.

一天早上，哈尔发现一半的狗粮已经吃完了。

They had only traveled a quarter of the total trail distance.

他们只走了总路程的四分之一。

No more food could be bought, no matter what price was offered.

无论出价多少，都买不到更多的食物。

He reduced the dogs' portions below the standard daily ration.

他将狗的食量减少到标准每日定量以下。

At the same time, he demanded longer travel to make up for loss.

同时，他要求延长旅行时间以弥补损失。

Mercedes and Charles supported this plan, but failed in execution.

梅赛德斯和查尔斯支持这个计划，但在执行上失败了。

Their heavy sled and lack of skill made progress nearly impossible.

由于雪橇太重，加上缺乏技巧，他们的前进几乎是不可能的。

It was easy to give less food, but impossible to force more effort.

少给食物很容易，但强迫别人多付出却不可能。

They couldn't start early, nor could they travel for extra hours.

他们不能早点出发，也不能加班。

They didn't know how to work the dogs, nor themselves, for that matter.

他们不知道该如何训练狗，甚至不知道该如何训练他们自己。

The first dog to die was Dub, the unlucky but hardworking thief.

第一只死去的狗是杜布，一只不幸但勤奋的小偷。

Though often punished, Dub had pulled his weight without complaint.

尽管经常受到惩罚，但杜布仍然毫无怨言地尽职尽责。

His injured shoulder grew worse without care or needed rest.

他的肩膀受伤，如果不加以治疗或休息，情况就会变得更糟。

Finally, Hal used the revolver to end Dub's suffering.

最后，哈尔用左轮手枪结束了杜布的痛苦。

A common saying claimed that normal dogs die on husky rations.

有句俗话说，普通的狗吃了哈士奇的食物就会死。

Buck's six new companions had only half the husky's share of food.

巴克的六个新伙伴只得到了哈士奇一半的食物份额。

The Newfoundland died first, then the three short-haired pointers.

纽芬兰犬首先死去，然后是三只短毛指针犬。

The two mongrels held on longer but finally perished like the rest.

两只杂种狗坚持得更久，但最终还是像其他狗一样死去了。

By this time, all the amenities and gentleness of the Southland were gone.

此时，南国的舒适与温柔已荡然无存。

The three people had shed the last traces of their civilized upbringing.

这三个人已经失去了文明成长的最后一丝痕迹。

Stripped of glamour and romance, Arctic travel became brutally real.

北极旅行失去了魅力和浪漫，变得残酷而真实。

It was a reality too harsh for their sense of manhood and womanhood.

对于他们的男子气概和女人味而言，这个现实太过残酷。

Mercedes no longer wept for the dogs, but now wept only for herself.

梅赛德斯不再为狗哭泣，现在只为自己哭泣。

She spent her time crying and quarreling with Hal and Charles.

她一直哭泣并与哈尔和查尔斯争吵。

Quarreling was the one thing they were never too tired to do.

争吵是他们永远不会厌倦的一件事。

Their irritability came from misery, grew with it, and surpassed it.

他们的烦躁源自痛苦，并随着痛苦而增长，最终超越痛苦。

The patience of the trail, known to those who toil and suffer kindly, never came.

那些辛勤劳作、忍受痛苦的人所知道的耐心之路从未到来。

That patience, which keeps speech sweet through pain, was unknown to them.

他们不知道，在痛苦中，耐心能让言语保持甜美。

They had no hint of patience, no strength drawn from suffering with grace.

他们没有一丝耐心，也没有从忍受痛苦中获得力量。

They were stiff with pain—aching in their muscles, bones, and hearts.

他们因疼痛而僵硬——肌肉、骨头和心脏都在疼痛。

Because of this, they grew sharp of tongue and quick with harsh words.
因此，他们的言辞变得尖刻，而且容易说出恶毒的话。

Each day began and ended with angry voices and bitter complaints.
每天的开始和结束都是在愤怒的声音和痛苦的抱怨中。

Charles and Hal wrangled whenever Mercedes gave them a chance.
只要梅赛德斯给他们机会，查尔斯和哈尔就会争吵起来。

Each man believed he did more than his fair share of the work.
每个人都认为自己所做的工作超过了自己应承担的份额。

Neither ever missed a chance to say so, again and again.
他们俩都不会错过一次又一次表达自己观点的机会。

Sometimes Mercedes sided with Charles, sometimes with Hal.
有时梅赛德斯站在查尔斯一边，有时站在哈尔一边。

This led to a grand and endless quarrel among the three.
这导致三人之间爆发了一场巨大而无休止的争吵。

A dispute over who should chop firewood grew out of control.
关于谁应该砍柴的争论愈演愈烈。

Soon, fathers, mothers, cousins, and dead relatives were named.
很快，父亲、母亲、表亲和已故亲属的名字就被列出来了。

Hal's views on art or his uncle's plays became part of the fight.
哈尔对艺术的看法或他叔叔的戏剧成为了争论的一部分。

Charles's political beliefs also entered the debate.
查尔斯的政治信仰也进入了争论之中。

To Mercedes, even her husband's sister's gossip seemed relevant.
对于梅赛德斯来说，就连她丈夫姐姐的八卦似乎也与她有关。

She aired opinions on that and on many of Charles's family's flaws.
她对此以及查尔斯家族的许多缺点发表了自己的看法。

While they argued, the fire stayed unlit and camp half set.
当他们争吵的时候，火还没有点燃，营地也只搭了一半。

Meanwhile, the dogs remained cold and without any food.
与此同时，狗仍然处于寒冷之中，并且没有任何食物。

Mercedes held a grievance she considered deeply personal.
梅赛德斯心里怀着深深的个人怨恨。

She felt mistreated as a woman, denied her gentle privileges.
她觉得自己作为一名女性受到了虐待，被剥夺了应有的温柔权利。

She was pretty and soft, and used to chivalry all her life.
她美丽而温柔，一生都具有骑士精神。

But her husband and brother now treated her with impatience.
但她的丈夫和兄弟现在对她很不耐烦。

Her habit was to act helpless, and they began to complain.
她习惯于表现得无助，于是他们开始抱怨。

Offended by this, she made their lives all the more difficult.
她因此而感到被冒犯，使他们的生活变得更加艰难。

She ignored the dogs and insisted on riding the sled herself.
她不理会狗，坚持自己骑雪橇。

Though light in looks, she weighed one hundred twenty pounds.

虽然看上去很轻盈，但她的体重却有一百二十磅。

That added burden was too much for the starving, weak dogs.

对于饥饿、虚弱的狗来说，额外的负担实在太重了。

Still, she rode for days, until the dogs collapsed in the reins.

尽管如此，她还是骑了好几天，直到狗在缰绳上倒下。

The sled stood still, and Charles and Hal begged her to walk.

雪橇停了下来，查尔斯和哈尔恳求她走一走。

They pleaded and entreated, but she wept and called them cruel.

他们苦苦哀求，但她却哭泣着说他们残忍。

On one occasion, they pulled her off the sled with sheer force and anger.

有一次，他们用蛮力和愤怒把她从雪橇上拉了下来。

They never tried again after what happened that time.

自从那次事件发生之后，他们就再也没有尝试过。

She went limp like a spoiled child and sat in the snow.

她像一个被宠坏的孩子一样瘫软地坐在雪地里。

They moved on, but she refused to rise or follow behind.

他们继续前行，任她拒绝起身或跟在后面。

After three miles, they stopped, returned, and carried her back.

走了三英里后，他们停下来，又返回，并把她抬了回来。

They reloaded her onto the sled, again using brute strength.

他们再次用蛮力将她抬到雪橇上。

In their deep misery, they were callous to the dogs' suffering.

在深深的痛苦中，他们对狗的痛苦无动于衷。

Hal believed one must get hardened and forced that belief on others.

哈尔认为一个人必须变得坚强,并将这种信念强加于他人。

He first tried to preach his philosophy to his sister
他首先尝试向他的妹妹宣扬他的哲学

and then, without success, he preached to his brother-in-law.
然后,他又向他的姐夫传道,但没有成功。

He had more success with the dogs, but only because he hurt them.
他在训狗方面取得了更大的成功,但这只是因为他伤害了它们。

At Five Fingers, the dog food ran out of food completely.
在 Five Fingers,狗粮已经完全吃完了。

A toothless old squaw sold a few pounds of frozen horse-hide
一个没有牙齿的老女人卖了几磅冷冻马皮

Hal traded his revolver for the dried horse-hide.
哈尔用他的左轮手枪换了一张干马皮。

The meat had come from starved horses of cattlemen months before.
这些肉来自几个月前牧场主饿死的马。

Frozen, the hide was like galvanized iron; tough and inedible.
冷冻后,兽皮就像镀锌的铁一样,坚硬且无法食用。

The dogs had to chew endlessly at the hide to eat it.
狗必须不停地咀嚼兽皮才能吃掉它。

But the leathery strings and short hair were hardly nourishment.
但坚韧的绳索和短毛几乎不能提供任何营养。

Most of the hide was irritating, and not food in any true sense.
大部分兽皮都具有刺激性,并且不是真正意义上的食物。

And through it all, Buck staggered at the front, like in a nightmare.

而在整个过程中，巴克在前面摇摇晃晃，就像在一场噩梦中一样。

He pulled when able; when not, he lay until whip or club raised him.

能拉的时候他就拉；不能拉的时候他就躺着，直到用鞭子或棍棒把他拉起来。

His fine, glossy coat had lost all stiffness and sheen it once had.

他那细腻光滑的皮毛已经失去了昔日的坚硬和光泽。

His hair hung limp, draggled, and clotted with dried blood from the blows.

他的头发松软、凌乱，上面沾满了被打后留下的干血。

His muscles shrank to cords, and his flesh pads were all worn away.

他的肌肉萎缩成条状，肉垫全部磨损。

Each rib, each bone showed clearly through folds of wrinkled skin.

每根肋骨、每根骨头都透过皱巴巴的皮肤清晰地显露出来。

It was heartbreaking, yet Buck's heart could not break.

这令人心碎，但巴克的心却无法破碎。

The man in the red sweater had tested that and proved it long ago.

穿红毛衣的男人很久以前就测试过并证明了这一点。

As it was with Buck, so it was with all his remaining teammates.

巴克的情况如此，他剩下的队友也同样如此。

There were seven in total, each one a walking skeleton of misery.

总共有七个，每一个都是行走的痛苦骷髅。

They had grown numb to lash, feeling only distant pain.

他们已经对鞭打麻木了，只感觉到遥远的痛苦。

Even sight and sound reached them faintly, as through a thick fog.

他们甚至连视觉和听觉都难以察觉，就像透过浓雾一样。

They were not half alive—they were bones with dim sparks inside.

它们不再是半死不活的——

它们只是骨头，里面却闪烁着微弱的火花。

When stopped, they collapsed like corpses, their sparks almost gone.

当它们停下来时，它们就像尸体一样倒下，身上的火花几乎消失了。

And when the whip or club struck again, the sparks fluttered weakly.

当鞭子或棍棒再次击打时，火花就会无力地闪烁。

Then they rose, staggered forward, and dragged their limbs ahead.

然后他们站起身，蹒跚地向前走去，拖着四肢。

One day kind Billee fell and could no longer rise at all.

有一天，善良的比利倒下了，再也站不起来了。

Hal had traded his revolver, so he used an axe to kill Billee instead.

哈尔已经换了他的左轮手枪，所以他用斧头杀死了比利。

He struck him on the head, then cut his body free and dragged it away.

他击打了那人的头部，然后把他的身体砍断并拖走。

Buck saw this, and so did the others; they knew death was near.

巴克看到了这一幕，其他人也看到了；他们知道死亡即将来临。

Next day Koona went, leaving just five dogs in the starving team.

第二天，库纳就走了，只留下五只饥饿的狗留在队伍里。

Joe, no longer mean, was too far gone to be aware of much at all.
乔不再那么卑鄙，但他已经完全失去了意识。

Pike, no longer faking his injury, was barely conscious.
派克不再假装受伤，几乎失去了意识。

Solleks, still faithful, mourned he had no strength to give.
索莱克斯仍然忠诚，他哀叹自己没有力量给予。

Teek was beaten most because he was fresher, but fading fast.
蒂克之所以遭受打击最为严重，是因为他体能较为充沛，但状态却很快下滑。

And Buck, still in the lead, no longer kept order or enforced it.
而巴克，仍然处于领先地位，不再维持秩序或执行秩序。

Half blind with weakness, Buck followed the trail by feel alone.
由于虚弱，巴克几乎失去了视力，只能凭感觉追踪。

It was beautiful spring weather, but none of them noticed it.
春天的天气真好，但他们却没有一个人注意到。

Each day the sun rose earlier and set later than before.
每天太阳都比以前升得更早，落得更晚。

By three in the morning, dawn had come; twilight lasted till nine.
凌晨三点，黎明到来；暮色一直持续到晚上九点。

The long days were filled with the full blaze of spring sunshine.
漫长的日子里，春日的阳光灿烂无比。

The ghostly silence of winter had changed into a warm murmur.
冬日里幽灵般的寂静已变成温暖的低语。

All the land was waking, alive with the joy of living things.
整片大地都苏醒了，充满了生机勃勃的欢乐。

The sound came from what had lain dead and still through winter.

这声音来自冬天里死寂的土地。

Now, those things moved again, shaking off the long frost sleep.

现在，那些东西又动了起来，摆脱了漫长的霜冻沉睡。

Sap was rising through the dark trunks of the waiting pine trees.

树液正从等待的松树的黑色树干中涌出。

Willows and aspens burst out bright young buds on each twig.

柳树和白杨树的每根小枝上都冒出了鲜艳的嫩芽。

Shrubs and vines put on fresh green as the woods came alive.

树林里充满了生机，灌木和藤蔓也披上了新的绿装。

Crickets chirped at night, and bugs crawled in daylight sun.

蟋蟀在夜晚鸣叫，虫子在白天阳光下爬行。

Partridges boomed, and woodpeckers knocked deep in the trees.

鹧鸪鸣叫，啄木鸟在树丛深处啄木。

Squirrels chattered, birds sang, and geese honked over the dogs.

松鼠叽叽喳喳，鸟儿歌唱，鹅在狗的叫声中鸣叫。

The wild-fowl came in sharp wedges, flying up from the south.

野禽成群结队，从南方飞来。

From every hillside came the music of hidden, rushing streams.

每座山坡上都传来隐秘的、奔腾的溪水的音乐。

All things thawed and snapped, bent and burst back into motion.

一切事物都解冻、断裂、弯曲，然后重新开始运动。

The Yukon strained to break the cold chains of frozen ice.

育空河竭尽全力挣脱冰冻冰层的束缚。

The ice melted underneath, while the sun melted it from above.

冰在下面融化，而太阳从上面融化它。

Air-holes opened, cracks spread, and chunks fell into the river.

气孔打开，裂缝扩大，大块碎石掉入河中。

Amid all this bursting and blazing life, the travelers staggered.

在这片生机勃勃、绚烂夺目的生命中，旅人们步履蹒跚。

Two men, a woman, and a pack of huskies walked like the dead.

两个男人、一个女人和一群哈士奇像死人一样行走。

The dogs were falling, Mercedes wept, but still rode the sled.

狗不断摔倒，梅赛德斯哭了，但仍然骑着雪橇。

Hal cursed weakly, and Charles blinked through watering eyes.

哈尔无力地咒骂了一句，查尔斯则眨着泪眼。

They stumbled into John Thornton's camp by White River's mouth.

他们跌跌撞撞地闯入了怀特河河口附近的约翰·桑顿的营地。

When they stopped, the dogs dropped flat, as if all struck dead.

当他们停下来时，狗就倒下了，好像全部死了一样。

Mercedes wiped her tears and looked across at John Thornton.

梅赛德斯擦干眼泪，看着约翰·桑顿。

Charles sat on a log, slowly and stiffly, aching from the trail.

查尔斯坐在一根圆木上，动作缓慢而僵硬，因为走了这么远的路而感到疼痛。

Hal did the talking as Thornton carved the end of an axe-handle.

当桑顿雕刻斧柄末端时，哈尔负责讲话。

He whittled birch wood and answered with brief, firm replies.

他削着桦木，并给出了简短而坚定的回答。

When asked, he gave advice, certain it wasn't going to be followed.

当被问及时，他给出了建议，但肯定不会被采纳。

Hal explained, "They told us the trail ice was dropping out."

哈尔解释说："他们告诉我们，路上的冰正在融化。"

"They said we should stay put—but we made it to White River."

"他们说我们应该留在原地——
但我们还是到达了白河。"

He ended with a sneering tone, as if to claim victory in hardship.

他最后用一种嘲讽的语气说道，仿佛在宣告苦难中的胜利。

"And they told you true," John Thornton answered Hal quietly.

"他们告诉你的是真的，"约翰·桑顿平静地回答哈尔。

"The ice may give way at any moment—it's ready to drop out."

"冰随时可能崩塌——它随时都会掉下来。"

"Only blind luck and fools could have made it this far alive."

"只有盲目的运气和傻瓜才能活着走到今天。"

"I tell you straight, I wouldn't risk my life for all Alaska's gold."

"我实话告诉你，我不会为了阿拉斯加的所有黄金而冒生命危险。"

"That's because you're not a fool, I suppose," Hal answered.

"我想那是因为你不是傻瓜，"哈尔回答道。

"All the same, we'll go on to Dawson." He uncoiled his whip.

"不管怎样，我们还是要去道森。"他解开了鞭子。

"Get up there, Buck! Hi! Get up! Go on!" he shouted harshly.
"快上来，巴克！嗨！起来！快！" 他厉声喊道。

Thornton kept whittling, knowing fools won't hear reason.
桑顿继续削木头，他知道傻瓜不会听道理。

To stop a fool was futile—and two or three fooled changed nothing.
阻止一个傻瓜是徒劳的——
两三个傻瓜被骗也改变不了什么。

But the team didn't move at the sound of Hal's command.
但听到哈尔的命令，队伍却没有动。

By now, only blows could make them rise and pull forward.
现在，只有打击才能让他们站起来并向前迈进。

The whip snapped again and again across the weakened dogs.
鞭子一次又一次地抽打着那些虚弱的狗。

John Thornton pressed his lips tightly and watched in silence.
约翰·桑顿紧闭双唇，默默地看着。

Solleks was the first to crawl to his feet under the lash.
索莱克斯第一个在鞭子下爬起来。

Then Teek followed, trembling. Joe yelped as he stumbled up.
蒂克也跟着他，浑身颤抖。乔踉跄着爬起来，发出一声尖叫。

Pike tried to rise, failed twice, then finally stood unsteadily.
派克尝试站起来，失败了两次，最后摇摇晃晃地站了起来。

But Buck lay where he had fallen, not moving at all this time.
但巴克躺在倒下的地方，一动不动。

The whip slashed him over and over, but he made no sound.
鞭子一遍遍地抽打着他，但他却没有发出任何声音。

He did not flinch or resist, simply remained still and quiet.
他没有退缩或反抗，只是保持静止和安静。

Thornton stirred more than once, as if to speak, but didn't.

桑顿动了好几次，似乎想说话，但又没有说。

His eyes grew wet, and still the whip cracked against Buck.

他的眼睛湿润了，但鞭子仍然抽打着巴克。

At last, Thornton began pacing slowly, unsure of what to do.

最后，桑顿开始慢慢地踱步，不知道该做什么。

It was the first time Buck had failed, and Hal grew furious.

这是巴克第一次失败，哈尔非常愤怒。

He threw down the whip and picked up the heavy club instead.

他扔掉鞭子，拿起沉重的棍棒。

The wooden club came down hard, but Buck still did not rise to move.

木棍重重地砸了下来，但巴克仍然没有起身动弹。

Like his teammates, he was too weak—but more than that.

和他的队友一样，他太弱了——但还不止于此。

Buck had decided not to move, no matter what came next.

巴克决定不管接下来发生什么，都不动。

He felt something dark and certain hovering just ahead.

他感觉到前方有某种黑暗而确定的东西在徘徊。

That dread had seized him as soon as he reached the riverbank.

他一到达河岸就感到恐惧。

The feeling had not left him since he felt the ice thin under his paws.

自从他感觉到爪子下的冰变薄以来，这种感觉就一直没有消失。

Something terrible was waiting—he felt it just down the trail.

某种可怕的事情正在等待着他——
他感觉到它就在小路的尽头。

He wasn't going to walk towards that terrible thing ahead

他不会走向前面那个可怕的东西

He was not going to obey any command that took him to that thing.

他不会服从任何带他去做那件事的命令。

The pain of the blows hardly touched him now—he was too far gone.

现在他几乎感觉不到打击的痛苦了——
他已经筋疲力尽了。

The spark of life flickered low, dimmed beneath each cruel strike.

生命的火花在每一次残酷的打击下都摇曳不定，变得暗淡。

His limbs felt distant; his whole body seemed to belong to another.

他的四肢感觉很遥远；他的整个身体似乎属于另一个人。

He felt a strange numbness as the pain faded out completely.

当疼痛完全消失时，他感到一种奇怪的麻木感。

From far away, he sensed he was being beaten, but barely knew.

从很远的地方，他就感觉到自己被打败了，但几乎不知道。

He could hear the thuds faintly, but they no longer truly hurt.

他能隐隐听到砰砰的声音，但已经不再感到疼痛了。

The blows landed, but his body no longer seemed like his own.

打击仍在，但他的身体似乎不再是他自己的了。

Then suddenly, without warning, John Thornton gave a wild cry.

突然，没有任何预兆，约翰·桑顿发出一声狂野的叫喊。

It was inarticulate, more the cry of a beast than of a man.

它的声音含糊不清，与其说是人的叫声，不如说是野兽的叫声。

He leapt at the man with the club and knocked Hal
backward.

他向手持棍棒的男子扑去，并将哈尔击退。

Hal flew as if struck by a tree, landing hard upon the
ground.

哈尔像被树击中一样飞了出去，重重地摔在地上。

Mercedes screamed aloud in panic and clutched at her face.

梅赛德斯惊慌地大声尖叫并捂住自己的脸。

Charles only looked on, wiped his eyes, and stayed seated.

查尔斯只是看着，擦了擦眼睛，然后坐着。

His body was too stiff with pain to rise or help in the fight.

他的身体因疼痛而僵硬，无法站起来或参与战斗。

Thornton stood over Buck, trembling with fury, unable to
speak.

桑顿站在巴克身边，气得浑身发抖，说不出话来。

He shook with rage and fought to find his voice through it.

他愤怒得浑身发抖，努力发出自己的声音。

"If you strike that dog again, I'll kill you," he finally said.

"如果你再打那条狗，我就杀了你，"他最后说道。

Hal wiped blood from his mouth and came forward again.

哈尔擦掉嘴上的血，再次走上前来。

"It's my dog," he muttered. "Get out of the way, or I'll fix
you."

"这是我的狗，"他低声说道，"走开，不然我就揍
你。"

"I'm going to Dawson, and you're not stopping me," he
added.

"我要去道森，你别阻止我，"他补充道。

Thornton stood firm between Buck and the angry young
man.

桑顿坚定地站在巴克和愤怒的年轻人之间。

He had no intention of stepping aside or letting Hal pass.

他没有让开或让哈尔过去的意思。

Hal pulled out his hunting knife, long and dangerous in
hand.

哈尔拔出手中那把又长又危险的猎刀。

Mercedes screamed, then cried, then laughed in wild hysteria.

梅赛德斯尖叫起来，然后哭泣，最后歇斯底里地大笑起来。

Thornton struck Hal's hand with his axe-handle, hard and fast.

桑顿用斧头柄猛烈而快速地击打哈尔的手。

The knife was knocked loose from Hal's grip and flew to the ground.

刀从哈尔手中脱落，飞落到地上。

Hal tried to pick the knife up, and Thornton rapped his knuckles again.

哈尔试图拿起刀，桑顿再次敲击他的指关节。

Then Thornton stooped down, grabbed the knife, and held it.

然后桑顿弯下腰，抓起刀，握住它。

With two quick chops of the axe-handle, he cut Buck's reins.

他用斧柄快速砍了两下，砍断了巴克的缰绳。

Hal had no fight left in him and stepped back from the dog.

哈尔再也没有抵抗的迹象，他从狗身边退了回去。

Besides, Mercedes needed both arms now to keep her upright.

此外，梅赛德斯现在需要双臂来保持直立。

Buck was too near death to be of use for pulling a sled again.

巴克已经濒临死亡，无法再拉雪橇了。

A few minutes later, they pulled out, heading down the river.

几分钟后，他们起航，顺流而下。

Buck raised his head weakly and watched them leave the bank.

巴克无力地抬起头，目送他们离开银行。

Pike led the team, with Solleks at the rear in the wheel spot.

派克（Pike）带领团队，索莱克斯（Solleks）则在队伍后方担任方向盘手。

Joe and Teek walked between, both limping with exhaustion.
乔和蒂克走在中间，两人都因疲惫而一瘸一拐。

Mercedes sat on the sled, and Hal gripped the long gee-pole.
梅赛德斯坐在雪橇上，哈尔则紧握着长长的北极熊杆。

Charles stumbled behind, his steps clumsy and uncertain.
查尔斯跌跌撞撞地跟在后面，脚步笨拙而蹒跚。

Thornton knelt by Buck and gently felt for broken bones.
桑顿跪在巴克身边，轻轻地摸索着他断裂的骨头。

His hands were rough but moved with kindness and care.
他的双手粗糙，却充满善良和关怀。

Buck's body was bruised but showed no lasting injury.
巴克的身体受了伤，但没有留下永久的伤痕。

What remained was terrible hunger and near-total weakness.
剩下的只有极度的饥饿和近乎完全的虚弱。

By the time this was clear, the sled had gone far downriver.
等到一切明朗起来时，雪橇已经顺着河流走了很远。

Man and dog watched the sled slowly crawl over the cracking ice.
男人和狗看着雪橇慢慢地爬过龟裂的冰面。

Then, they saw the sled sink down into a hollow.
然后，他们看到雪橇陷入了一个凹陷中。

The gee-pole flew up, with Hal still clinging to it in vain.
导航杆飞了起来，哈尔仍然徒劳地抓住它。

Mercedes's scream reached them across the cold distance.
梅赛德斯的尖叫声穿过寒冷的距离传到了他们耳中。

Charles turned and stepped back—but he was too late.
查尔斯转身向后退——但是已经太迟了。

A whole ice sheet gave way, and they all dropped through.
整个冰盖崩塌了，他们都掉了下去。

Dogs, sled, and people vanished into the black water below.
狗、雪橇和人们都消失在下面的黑色水中。

Only a wide hole in the ice was left where they had passed.

他们经过的地方，冰面上只留下了一个大洞。

The trail's bottom had dropped out—just as Thornton warned.

正如桑顿警告的那样，小路的底部已经塌陷。

Thornton and Buck looked at one another, silent for a moment.

桑顿和巴克互相看了一眼，沉默了一会儿。

"You poor devil," said Thornton softly, and Buck licked his hand.

"你这个可怜的家伙，"桑顿轻声说道，巴克舔了舔他的手。

For the Love of a Man
《为了男人的爱》

John Thornton froze his feet in the cold of the previous December.
去年 12 月的寒冷让约翰·桑顿的脚冻伤了。

His partners made him comfortable and left him to recover alone.
他的伙伴们让他感到舒适并让他独自康复。

They went up the river to gather a raft of saw-logs for Dawson.
他们沿河而上，为道森收集了一筏锯木。

He was still limping slightly when he rescued Buck from death.
当他把巴克从死亡线上救回来时，他仍然有些跛行。

But with warm weather continuing, even that limp disappeared.
但随着天气持续变暖，连那种跛行也消失了。

Lying by the riverbank during long spring days, Buck rested.
漫长的春日里，巴克躺在河岸边休息。

He watched the flowing water and listened to birds and insects.
他看着流水，聆听鸟鸣虫叫。

Slowly, Buck regained his strength under the sun and sky.
在阳光和天空的照耀下，巴克慢慢地恢复了体力。

A rest felt wonderful after traveling three thousand miles.
旅途三千里之后，休息一下感觉真好。

Buck became lazy as his wounds healed and his body filled out.
随着伤口的愈合和身体的长大，巴克变得懒惰起来。

His muscles grew firm, and flesh returned to cover his bones.
他的肌肉变得结实，血肉重新覆盖住他的骨头。

They were all resting—Buck, Thornton, Skeet, and Nig.

他们都在休息——巴克、桑顿、斯基特和尼格。

They waited for the raft that was going to carry them down to Dawson.

他们等待着载他们去道森的木筏。

Skeet was a small Irish setter who made friends with Buck.

斯基特是一只小爱尔兰塞特犬，它和巴克是好朋友。

Buck was too weak and ill to resist her at their first meeting.

第一次见面时，巴克因身体虚弱、病情严重而无法拒绝她。

Skeet had the healer trait that some dogs naturally possess.

斯基特具有某些狗天生具有的治疗特质。

Like a mother cat, she licked and cleaned Buck's raw wounds.

就像一只母猫一样，她舔舐并清理巴克的伤口。

Every morning after breakfast, she repeated her careful work.

每天早晨吃完早餐后，她又重复着细致的工作。

Buck came to expect her help as much as he did Thornton's.

巴克开始期待她的帮助，就像他期待桑顿的帮助一样。

Nig was friendly too, but less open and less affectionate.

Nig 也很友好，但不太开放，也不太热情。

Nig was a big black dog, part bloodhound and part deerhound.

尼格是一只大黑狗，一半是猎犬，一半是猎鹿犬。

He had laughing eyes and endless good nature in his spirit.

他有着爱笑的眼睛和无尽的善良。

To Buck's surprise, neither dog showed jealousy toward him.

令巴克惊讶的是，两只狗都没有对他表现出嫉妒。

Both Skeet and Nig shared the kindness of John Thornton.

Skeet 和 Nig 都秉承了 John Thornton 的善良。

As Buck got stronger, they lured him into foolish dog games.

随着巴克变得越来越强壮，他们引诱他参与愚蠢的狗游戏。

Thornton often played with them too, unable to resist their joy.

桑顿也经常和它们一起玩耍，无法抗拒它们的快乐。

In this playful way, Buck moved from illness to a new life.

巴克就这样嬉戏的方式从病痛中走向了新生。

Love—true, burning, and passionate love—was his at last.

他终于得到了爱情——真挚、炽热、热烈的爱情。

He had never known this kind of love at Miller's estate.

他在米勒的庄园里从未感受到过这种爱。

With the Judge's sons, he had shared work and adventure.

他与法官的儿子们一起工作、一起冒险。

With the grandsons, he saw stiff and boastful pride.

在这些孙子身上，他看到了僵硬而自负的骄傲。

With Judge Miller himself, he had a respectful friendship.

他与米勒法官本人保持着令人尊敬的友谊。

But love that was fire, madness, and worship came with Thornton.

但桑顿却对爱情充满了热情、疯狂和崇拜。

This man had saved Buck's life, and that alone meant a great deal.

这个人救了巴克的命，仅此一点就意义重大。

But more than that, John Thornton was the ideal kind of master.

但更重要的是，约翰·桑顿是一位理想的大师。

Other men cared for dogs out of duty or business necessity.

其他人则出于职责或业务需要而照顾狗。

John Thornton cared for his dogs as if they were his children.

约翰·桑顿照顾他的狗就像照顾自己的孩子一样。

He cared for them because he loved them and simply could not help it.

他关心他们，因为他爱他们，而且他根本就无法控制自己。

John Thornton saw even further than most men ever managed to see.

约翰·桑顿的眼光比大多数人看得更远。

He never forgot to greet them kindly or speak a cheering word.

他从不忘记热情地问候他们，或者说一句鼓励的话。

He loved sitting down with the dogs for long talks, or "gassy," as he said.

他喜欢和狗坐在一起长谈，或者用他的话说，"聊聊天"。

He liked to seize Buck's head roughly between his strong hands.

他喜欢用强壮的手粗鲁地抓住巴克的头。

Then he rested his own head against Buck's and shook him gently.

然后他把自己的头靠在巴克的头上，轻轻地摇晃着他。

All the while, he called Buck rude names that meant love to Buck.

他一直用粗鲁的名字辱骂巴克，但对巴克来说，这其实是爱。

To Buck, that rough embrace and those words brought deep joy.

对于巴克来说，那个粗暴的拥抱和那些话语给他带来了深深的快乐。

His heart seemed to shake loose with happiness at each movement.

他的每一个动作都让他的心快乐得仿佛要跳起来。

When he sprang up afterward, his mouth looked like it laughed.

当他随后跳起来时，他的嘴看起来像是在笑。

His eyes shone brightly and his throat trembled with unspoken joy.

他的眼睛闪闪发光，喉咙因无言的喜悦而颤抖。

His smile stood still in that state of emotion and glowing affection.

在那种激动和炽热的爱意中，他的笑容静止不动。

Then Thornton exclaimed thoughtfully, "God! he can almost speak!"

然后桑顿若有所思地惊呼道："天哪！他几乎能说话了！"

Buck had a strange way of expressing love that nearly caused pain.

巴克表达爱的方式很奇怪，几乎会造成痛苦。

He often griped Thornton's hand in his teeth very tightly.

他经常用牙齿紧紧咬住桑顿的手。

The bite was going to leave deep marks that stayed for some time after.

咬伤会留下深深的痕迹，并且会持续一段时间。

Buck believed those oaths were love, and Thornton knew the same.

巴克相信这些誓言就是爱，桑顿也这么认为。

Most often, Buck's love showed in quiet, almost silent adoration.

大多数时候，巴克的爱表现为安静、几乎无声的崇拜。

Though thrilled when touched or spoken to, he did not seek attention.

尽管当被触摸或被说话时他很兴奋，但他并不寻求关注。

Skeet nudged her nose under Thornton's hand until he petted her.

斯基特用鼻子轻轻推着桑顿的手，直到他抚摸她。

Nig walked up quietly and rested his large head on Thornton's knee.

尼格静静地走上前去，将他的大脑袋靠在桑顿的膝盖上。

Buck, in contrast, was satisfied to love from a respectful distance.
相比之下，巴克满足于保持距离去爱。

He lied for hours at Thornton's feet, alert and watching closely.
他连续几个小时躺在桑顿的脚边，保持警惕并密切观察。

Buck studied every detail of his master's face and slightest motion.
巴克仔细观察主人脸上的每一个细节和最细微的动作。

Or lied farther away, studying the man's shape in silence.
或者躺在更远的地方，默默地观察着那个男人的身影。

Buck watched each small move, each shift in posture or gesture.
巴克观察着每一个细微的动作、每一个姿势或手势的变化。

So powerful was this connection that often pulled Thornton's gaze.
这种联系如此强大，常常吸引桑顿的目光。

He met Buck's eyes with no words, love shining clearly through.
他无言地看着巴克的眼睛，眼中却闪耀着爱意。

For a long while after being saved, Buck never let Thornton out of sight.
获救后很长一段时间，巴克都没有让桑顿离开他的视线。

Whenever Thornton left the tent, Buck followed him closely outside.
每当桑顿离开帐篷时，巴克都会紧紧跟随他出去。

All the harsh masters in the Northland had made Buck afraid to trust.
北国所有严酷的主人都让巴克不敢相信。

He feared no man could remain his master for more than a short time.

他担心没有人能够长期担任他的主人。

He feared John Thornton was going to vanish like Perrault and François.

他担心约翰·桑顿会像佩罗和弗朗索瓦一样消失。

Even at night, the fear of losing him haunted Buck's restless sleep.

甚至在晚上,失去他的恐惧仍然困扰着巴克不安的睡眠。

When Buck woke, he crept out into the cold, and went to the tent.

巴克醒来后,便蹑手蹑脚地走进寒冷的帐篷。

He listened carefully for the soft sound of breathing inside.

他仔细聆听里面轻微的呼吸声。

Despite Buck's deep love for John Thornton, the wild stayed alive.

尽管巴克深爱着约翰·桑顿,但荒野依然存在。

That primitive instinct, awakened in the North, did not disappear.

在北方被唤醒的原始本能并没有消失。

Love brought devotion, loyalty, and the fire-side's warm bond.

爱情带来奉献、忠诚和炉边的温暖纽带。

But Buck also kept his wild instincts, sharp and ever alert.

但巴克也保留着他的野性本能,敏锐而警惕。

He was not just a tamed pet from the soft lands of civilization.

他不仅仅是一只来自文明柔软土地的驯服宠物。

Buck was a wild being who had come in to sit by Thornton's fire.

巴克是个野人,他来到桑顿的火堆旁坐着。

He looked like a Southland dog, but wildness lived within him.

他看上去像一条南国狗,但内心却充满野性。

His love for Thornton was too great to allow theft from the man.

他对桑顿的爱太深了，他不允许桑顿偷窃他的东西。

But in any other camp, he would steal boldly and without pause.

但在任何其他营地，他都会大胆地、毫不犹豫地偷窃。

He was so clever in stealing that no one could catch or accuse him.

他偷窃非常聪明，所以没有人能抓住他或指控他。

His face and body were covered in scars from many past fights.

他的脸上和身上布满了过去多次战斗留下的伤疤。

Buck still fought fiercely, but now he fought with more cunning.

巴克的战斗依然凶猛，但现在他的战斗更加狡猾。

Skeet and Nig were too gentle to fight, and they were Thornton's.

Skeet 和 Nig 性格太温和，不适合打架，而且他们是 Thornton 的。

But any strange dog, no matter how strong or brave, gave way.

但任何陌生的狗，无论多么强壮或勇敢，都会屈服。

Otherwise, the dog found itself battling Buck; fighting for its life.

否则，这只狗就会发现自己正在与巴克搏斗；为自己的生命而战。

Buck had no mercy once he chose to fight against another dog.

一旦巴克选择与另一只狗打架，它就不会留情面。

He had learned well the law of club and fang in the Northland.

他在北国已经很好地学会了棍棒和尖牙的法则。

He never gave up an advantage and never backed away from battle.

他从不放弃优势，也从不退缩。

He had studied Spitz and the fiercest dogs of mail and police.

他研究过斯皮茨犬以及最凶猛的邮犬和警犬。

He knew clearly there was no middle ground in wild combat.

他很清楚，野外战斗中没有中间地带。

He must rule or be ruled; showing mercy meant showing weakness.

他必须统治，否则就被统治；表现出仁慈就意味着表现出软弱。

Mercy was unknown in the raw and brutal world of survival.

在残酷而原始的生存世界中，仁慈是不存在的。

To show mercy was seen as fear, and fear led quickly to death.

表现出仁慈会被视为恐惧，而恐惧很快就会导致死亡。

The old law was simple: kill or be killed, eat or be eaten.

旧法律很简单：杀或被杀，吃或被吃。

That law came from the depths of time, and Buck followed it fully.

这条法则源自时间的深处，而巴克也完全遵循了它。

Buck was older than his years and the number of breaths he took.

巴克的年龄比他的实际年龄和呼吸次数要大。

He connected the ancient past with the present moment clearly.

他将古老的过去与现在清晰地联系在一起。

The deep rhythms of the ages moved through him like the tides.

时代的深沉韵律如同潮水般涌过他的心头。

Time pulsed in his blood as surely as seasons moved the earth.

时间在他的血液中跳动，就如季节在地球上移动一样。

He sat by Thornton's fire, strong-chested and white-fanged.

他坐在桑顿的火堆旁，胸膛强健，牙齿洁白。

His long fur waved, but behind him the spirits of wild dogs watched.

他的长毛飘扬，但在他身后，野狗的灵魂注视着他。

Half-wolves and full wolves stirred within his heart and senses.

半狼与全狼在他的内心和感官中激荡。

They tasted his meat and drank the same water that he did.

他们尝了他的肉，喝了和他一样的水。

They sniffed the wind alongside him and listened to the forest.

他们和他一起嗅着风的气息，聆听着森林的声音。

They whispered the meanings of the wild sounds in the darkness.

他们在黑暗中低声诉说着野外声音的含义。

They shaped his moods and guided each of his quiet reactions.

它们塑造了他的情绪并引导他的每一个安静的反应。

They lay with him as he slept and became part of his deep dreams.

它们在他睡觉时陪伴着他，成为他深梦的一部分。

They dreamed with him, beyond him, and made up his very spirit.

他们与他一起做梦，超越他，构成了他的精神。

The spirits of the wild called so strongly that Buck felt pulled.

野性之灵的召唤如此强烈，巴克感觉自己被拉扯着。

Each day, mankind and its claims grew weaker in Buck's heart.

在巴克的心里，人类和人类的诉求一天天变得越来越薄弱。

Deep in the forest, a strange and thrilling call was going to rise.

森林深处，一阵诡异而又惊心动魄的呼唤即将响起。

Every time he heard the call, Buck felt an urge he could not resist.

每次听到这个呼唤，巴克就会感到一种无法抗拒的冲动。

He was going to turn from the fire and from the beaten human paths.

他要远离火海，远离人间的道路。

He was going to plunge into the forest, going forward without knowing why.

他就要冲进森林，不知道为什么就向前走去。

He did not question this pull, for the call was deep and powerful.

他没有质疑这种吸引力，因为这种吸引力深沉而强大。

Often, he reached the green shade and soft untouched earth

他常常到达绿荫和柔软的、未被触及的土地

But then the strong love for John Thornton pulled him back to the fire.

但随后对约翰·桑顿的强烈爱意又把他拉回到了火堆旁。

Only John Thornton truly held Buck's wild heart in his grasp.

只有约翰·桑顿真正掌握了巴克狂野的心。

The rest of mankind had no lasting value or meaning to Buck.

其余人类对巴克来说没有任何持久的价值或意义。

Strangers might praise him or stroke his fur with friendly hands.

陌生人可能会称赞他或用友好的手抚摸他的皮毛。

Buck remained unmoved and walked off from too much affection.

巴克不为所动，因受到过多的爱抚而走开了。

Hans and Pete arrived with the raft that had long been awaited

汉斯和皮特带着期待已久的木筏来了

Buck ignored them until he learned they were close to Thornton.

巴克一直没有理会他们，直到他得知他们离桑顿很近。

After that, he tolerated them, but never showed them full warmth.

此后，他容忍了他们，但从未向他们表现出完全的热情。

He took food or kindness from them as if doing them a favor.

他接受他们的食物或善意，就好像在给他们做一件好事一样。

They were like Thornton—simple, honest, and clear in thought.

他们就像桑顿一样——单纯、诚实、思维清晰。

All together they traveled to Dawson's saw-mill and the great eddy

他们一起去了道森的锯木厂和大漩涡

On their journey the learned to understand Buck's nature deeply.

在旅途中，他们深刻理解了巴克的本性。

They did not try to grow close like Skeet and Nig had done.

他们并没有像 Skeet 和 Nig 那样试图变得亲密。

But Buck's love for John Thornton only deepened over time.

但巴克对约翰·桑顿的爱随着时间的推移而加深。

Only Thornton could place a pack on Buck's back in the summer.

只有桑顿能够在夏天把背包放在巴克的背上。

Whatever Thornton commanded, Buck was willing to do fully.

无论桑顿命令什么，巴克都愿意完全执行。

One day, after they left Dawson for the headwaters of the Tanana,

有一天，他们离开道森前往塔纳纳河源头后，

the group sat on a cliff that dropped three feet to bare bedrock.

这群人坐在一处悬崖上，悬崖下三英尺，露出裸露的基岩。

John Thornton sat near the edge, and Buck rested beside him.

约翰·桑顿坐在边缘附近，巴克在他旁边休息。

Thornton had a sudden thought and called the men's attention.

桑顿突然想到一个主意，并引起了人们的注意。

He pointed across the chasm and gave Buck a single command.

他指着峡谷对面，向巴克发出了一个简单的命令。

"Jump, Buck!" he said, swinging his arm out over the drop.

"跳，巴克！"他一边说，一边把手臂挥向悬崖。

In a moment, he had to grab Buck, who was leaping to obey.

一会儿，他必须抓住巴克，巴克正跳起来服从命令。

Hans and Pete rushed forward and pulled both back to safety.

汉斯和皮特冲上前去，把两人拉回了安全地带。

After all ended, and they had caught their breath, Pete spoke up.

一切结束后，他们都松了一口气，皮特开口说话了。

"The love's uncanny," he said, shaken by the dog's fierce devotion.

"这种爱太不可思议了，"他说道，这只狗的强烈忠诚让他很感动。

Thornton shook his head and replied with calm seriousness.

桑顿摇摇头，平静而严肃地回答道。

"No, the love is splendid," he said, "but also terrible."
"不，爱情很美好，"他说，"但也很可怕。"

"Sometimes, I must admit, this kind of love makes me afraid."
"有时候，我必须承认，这种爱让我害怕。"

Pete nodded and said. "I'd hate to be the man who touches you."
皮特点点头，说道："我可不想成为那个碰你的人。"

He looked at Buck as he spoke, serious and full of respect.
他说话时看着巴克，严肃而充满敬意。

"Py Jingo!" said Hans quickly. "Me either, no sir."
"Py Jingo！"汉斯赶紧说道，"我也是，不，先生。"

Before the year ended, Pete's fears came true at Circle City.
年底之前，皮特的担忧在 Circle City 变成了现实。

A cruel man named Black Burton picked a fight in the bar.
一个名叫布莱克·伯顿的残忍男人在酒吧里挑起斗殴。

He was angry and malicious, lashing out at a new tenderfoot.
他愤怒又恶毒，对一个新手大发雷霆。

John Thornton stepped in, calm and good-natured as always.
约翰·桑顿走了进来，一如既往地冷静和善良。

Buck lay in a corner, head down, watching Thornton closely.
巴克躺在角落里，低着头，仔细地注视着桑顿。

Burton suddenly struck, his punch sending Thornton spinning.
伯顿突然出击，一拳将桑顿打得天旋地转。

Only the bar's rail kept him from crashing hard to the ground.
只有酒吧的扶手才能阻止他重重地摔到地面。

The watchers heard a sound that was not bark or yelp
观察者听到了一种既不是吠叫也不是尖叫的声音

a deep roar came from Buck as he launched toward the man.
巴克向那人冲去，发出一声低沉的吼叫。

Burton threw his arm up and barely saved his own life.
伯顿举起手臂，险些保住了性命。

Buck crashed into him, knocking him flat onto the floor.
巴克撞到他，把他撞倒在地。

Buck bit deep into the man's arm, then lunged for the throat.
巴克深深咬住那人的手臂，然后猛扑向他的喉咙。

Burton could only partly block, and his neck was torn open.
伯顿只能部分阻挡，脖子被撕开。

Men rushed in, clubs raised, and drove Buck off the bleeding man.
人们冲进来，举起棍棒，把巴克从流血的男人身上赶了开来。

A surgeon worked quickly to stop the blood from flowing out.
外科医生迅速采取行动，止住血液流出。

Buck paced and growled, trying to attack again and again.
巴克一边踱步一边咆哮，试图一次又一次地发起攻击。

Only swinging clubs kept him back from reaching Burton.
只有挥舞的棍棒才能阻止他到达伯顿。

A miners' meeting was called and held right there on the spot.
矿工大会就地召开。

They agreed Buck had been provoked and voted to set him free.
他们一致认为巴克是受到了挑衅，并投票决定释放他。

But Buck's fierce name now echoed in every camp in Alaska.
但巴克凶猛的名字如今已在阿拉斯加的每个营地中回荡。

Later that fall, Buck saved Thornton again in a new way.
那年秋天晚些时候，巴克再次以一种新的方式拯救了
桑顿。

The three men were guiding a long boat down rough rapids.
这三个人正驾驶着一艘长船顺着湍急的河道前行。

Thornton maned the boat, calling directions to the shoreline.
桑顿掌着舵，向海岸线发出指示。

Hans and Pete ran on land, holding a rope from tree to tree.
汉斯和皮特在陆地上奔跑，抓着绳子从一棵树跑到另
一棵树。

Buck kept pace on the bank, always watching his master.
巴克在河岸上不停地行走，始终注视着他的主人。

At one nasty place, rocks jutted out under the fast water.
在一个令人讨厌的地方，岩石在湍急的水流下突出。

Hans let go of the rope, and Thornton steered the boat wide.
汉斯松开了绳子，桑顿把船驶向了远处。

Hans sprinted to catch the boat again past the dangerous
rocks.
汉斯冲过危险的岩石，再次赶上船。

The boat cleared the ledge but hit a stronger part of the
current.
船越过了岩架，但撞上了更强的水流。

Hans grabbed the rope too quickly and pulled the boat off
balance.
汉斯抓住绳子太快，导致船失去平衡。

The boat flipped over and slammed into the bank, bottom
up.
船翻了，船底朝天地撞上了岸。

Thornton was thrown out and swept into the wildest part of
the water.
桑顿被抛出水面并被卷入水面最险恶的地方。

No swimmer could have survived in those deadly, racing
waters.

没有任何游泳者能够在这些致命的湍急水域中生存下来。

Buck jumped in instantly and chased his master down the river.

巴克立即跳入水中，追着主人顺着河而下。

After three hundred yards, he reached Thornton at last.

走了三百码后，他终于到达了桑顿。

Thornton grabbed Buck's tail, and Buck turned for the shore.

桑顿抓住了巴克的尾巴，巴克转身向岸边游去。

He swam with full strength, fighting the water's wild drag.

他拼尽全力游着，抵抗着水的猛烈阻力。

They moved downstream faster than they could reach the shore.

他们顺流而下的速度比到达岸边的速度还快。

Ahead, the river roared louder as it fell into deadly rapids.

前方，河水咆哮声越来越大，形成致命的急流。

Rocks sliced through the water like the teeth of a huge comb.

岩石像一把巨大梳子的齿一样划破水面。

The pull of the water near the drop was savage and inescapable.

靠近落差处的水的拉力是巨大而无法避免的。

Thornton knew they could never make the shore in time.

桑顿知道他们不可能及时到达岸边。

He scraped over one rock, smashed across a second,

他刮过一块岩石，又撞上另一块，

And then he crashed into a third rock, grabbing it with both hands.

然后他撞上了第三块岩石，用双手抓住了它。

He let go of Buck and shouted over the roar, "Go, Buck! Go!"

他放开巴克，大声喊道："快，巴克！快！"

Buck could not stay afloat and was swept down by the current.

巴克无法浮在水面上，被水流冲走了。

He fought hard, struggling to turn, but made no headway at all.

他拼命挣扎，挣扎着转身，但却毫无进展。

Then he heard Thornton repeat the command over the river's roar.

然后他听到桑顿在河水的咆哮声中重复了命令。

Buck reared out of the water, raised his head as if for a last look.

巴克从水里站了起来，抬起头，仿佛要看最后一眼。

then turned and obeyed, swimming toward the bank with resolve.

然后转身服从，坚决地向岸边游去。

Pete and Hans pulled him ashore at the final possible moment.

皮特和汉斯在最后一刻将他拉上了岸。

They knew Thornton could cling to the rock for only minutes more.

他们知道桑顿只能坚持在岩石上几分钟。

They ran up the bank to a spot far above where he was hanging.

他们沿着河岸跑去，来到比他悬挂的地方高得多的地方。

They tied the boat's line to Buck's neck and shoulders carefully.

他们小心翼翼地将船绳系在巴克的脖子和肩膀上。

The rope was snug but loose enough for breathing and movement.

绳子很紧，但又足够松，方便呼吸和活动。

Then they launched him into the rushing, deadly river again.

然后他们又把他扔进了湍急而致命的河流。

Buck swam boldly but missed his angle into the stream's force.

巴克大胆地游着，但却没有游进湍急的水流中。

He saw too late that he was going to drift past Thornton.

他意识到自己即将超越桑顿，但为时已晚。

Hans jerked the rope tight, as if Buck were a capsizing boat.

汉斯猛地拉紧绳子，仿佛巴克是一艘倾覆的小船。

The current pulled him under, and he vanished below the surface.

水流将他拉下水，他消失在水面之下。

His body struck the bank before Hans and Pete pulled him out.

在汉斯和皮特将他拉出来之前，他的身体撞到了岸边。

He was half-drowned, and they pounded the water out of him.

他已经半溺水了，他们把他体内的水打出来。

Buck stood, staggered, and collapsed again onto the ground.

巴克站起来，踉跄了一下，再次倒在地上。

Then they heard Thornton's voice faintly carried by the wind.

然后他们听到风中隐隐传来桑顿的声音。

Though the words were unclear, they knew he was near death.

虽然话语不清楚，但他们知道他已经快要死了。

The sound of Thornton's voice hit Buck like an electric jolt.

桑顿的声音让巴克如遭电击。

He jumped up and ran up the bank, returning to the launch point.

他跳起来，跑上河岸，回到了出发点。

Again they tied the rope to Buck, and again he entered the stream.

他们再次将绳子绑在巴克身上，他再次跳入小溪。

This time, he swam directly and firmly into the rushing water.

这一次，他直接、坚定地游进了湍急的水流中。

Hans let out the rope steadily while Pete kept it from tangling.

汉斯稳稳地放出绳子，而皮特则负责防止绳子缠结。

Buck swam hard until he was lined up just above Thornton.

巴克奋力游动，直到他位于桑顿正上方。

Then he turned and charged down like a train in full speed.

然后他转身，像一列全速的火车一样冲了下去。

Thornton saw him coming, braced, and locked arms around his neck.

桑顿看到他来了，做好了准备，用双臂搂住他的脖子。

Hans tied the rope fast around a tree as both were pulled under.

汉斯将绳子紧紧地绑在一棵树上，然后把两人都拉下去。

They tumbled underwater, smashing into rocks and river debris.

它们在水下翻滚，撞上岩石和河流碎片。

One moment Buck was on top, the next Thornton rose gasping.

前一刻巴克还在他上面，下一刻桑顿就气喘吁吁地站了起来。

Battered and choking, they veered to the bank and safety.

他们伤痕累累、窒息而亡，只好转向岸边寻求安全。

Thornton regained consciousness, lying across a drift log.

桑顿恢复了意识，躺在一根漂流木上。

Hans and Pete worked him hard to bring back breath and life.

汉斯和皮特努力帮助他恢复呼吸和生命。

His first thought was for Buck, who lay motionless and limp.

他首先想到的是巴克，它一动不动地躺在那里。

Nig howled over Buck's body, and Skeet licked his face gently.

尼格对着巴克的身体嚎叫，斯基特轻轻地舔着巴克的脸。

Thornton, sore and bruised, examined Buck with careful hands.

桑顿浑身酸痛，浑身瘀伤，他用手小心翼翼地检查巴克。

He found three ribs broken, but no deadly wounds in the dog.

他发现这只狗有三根肋骨断裂，但没有致命伤。

"That settles it," Thornton said. "We camp here." And they did.

"那就这么定了，"桑顿说。"我们就在这里扎营。"他们就真的扎营了。

They stayed until Buck's ribs healed and he could walk again.

他们一直待到巴克的肋骨痊愈并能再次行走。

That winter, Buck performed a feat that raised his fame further.

那年冬天，巴克完成了一项壮举，进一步提高了他的名气。

It was less heroic than saving Thornton, but just as impressive.

这虽然不如拯救桑顿那么英勇，但同样令人印象深刻。

At Dawson, the partners needed supplies for a distant journey.

在道森，合作伙伴需要为长途旅行提供补给。

They wanted to travel East, into untouched wilderness lands.

他们想前往东部，进入未被开发的荒野地区。

Buck's deed in the Eldorado Saloon made that trip possible.

巴克在埃尔多拉多酒吧的行为使得这次旅行成为可能。

It began with men bragging about their dogs over drinks.

事情的起因是，男人们边喝酒边吹嘘自己的狗。

Buck's fame made him the target of challenges and doubt.

巴克的名气使他成为挑战和怀疑的对象。

Thornton, proud and calm, stood firm in defending Buck's name.

桑顿骄傲而冷静，坚定地捍卫巴克的名字。

One man said his dog could pull five hundred pounds with ease.

一名男子说他的狗可以轻松拉动五百磅的重物。

Another said six hundred, and a third bragged seven hundred.

另一个人说有六百人，第三个人则夸口有七百人。

"Pfft!" said John Thornton, "Buck can pull a thousand pound sled."

"噗！"约翰·桑顿说，"巴克能拉动一千磅重的雪橇。"

Matthewson, a Bonanza King, leaned forward and challenged him.

富矿之王马修森倾身向前，向他发起挑战。

"You think he can put that much weight into motion?"

"你认为他能举起那么大的重量吗？"

"And you think he can pull the weight a full hundred yards?"

"你认为他能把重物拉出足足一百码吗？"

Thornton replied coolly, "Yes. Buck is dog enough to do it."

桑顿冷冷地回答："是的。巴克足够厉害，可以做到。"

"He'll put a thousand pounds into motion, and pull it a hundred yards."

"他会施加一千磅的力，然后把它拉一百码。"

Matthewson smiled slowly and made sure all men heard his words.

马修森慢慢地笑了笑，确保所有人都听到了他的话。

"I've got a thousand dollars that says he can't. There it is."

"我有一千美元可以证明他不行。就是这样。"

He slammed a sack of gold dust the size of sausage on the bar.

他把一袋香肠大小的金粉重重地扔在吧台上。

Nobody said a word. The silence grew heavy and tense around them.

没人说话。四周的寂静愈发沉重、紧张。

Thornton's bluff—if it was one—had been taken seriously.

桑顿的虚张声势——如果算的话——

已经被认真对待了。

He felt heat rise in his face as blood rushed to his cheeks.

他感到脸上发热，血液涌上脸颊。

His tongue had gotten ahead of his reason in that moment.

那一刻，他的舌头已经超越了他的理智。

He truly didn't know if Buck could move a thousand pounds.

他真的不知道巴克是否能搬动一千磅的重量。

Half a ton! The size of it alone made his heart feel heavy.

半吨！光是看着它的大小，就让他心里沉重无比。

He had faith in Buck's strength and had thought him capable.

他相信巴克的力量并且认为他有能力。

But he had never faced this kind of challenge, not like this.

但他从来没有面临过这种挑战，不是这样的。

A dozen men watched him quietly, waiting to see what he'd do.

十几个人静静地注视着他，等着看他要做什么。

He didn't have the money—neither did Hans or Pete.

他没有钱——汉斯和皮特也没有。

"I've got a sled outside," said Matthewson coldly and direct.

"我外面有一辆雪橇，" 马修森冷冷地直接说道。

"It's loaded with twenty sacks, fifty pounds each, all flour.

"里面装了二十袋面粉，每袋五十磅。

So don't let a missing sled be your excuse now," he added.

所以现在不要让雪橇丢失成为你的借口，" 他补充道
。

Thornton stood silent. He didn't know what words to offer.

桑顿沉默不语，不知道该说什么。

He looked around at the faces without seeing them clearly.
他环顾四周，但没看清楚他们的脸。

He looked like a man frozen in thought, trying to restart.
他看上去就像一个陷入沉思的人，试图重新开始。

Then he saw Jim O'Brien, a friend from the Mastodon days.
然后他见到了吉姆·奥布莱恩（Jim O'Brien），他是 Mastodon 时期的朋友。

That familiar face gave him courage he didn't know he had.
那张熟悉的面孔给了他从未意识到的勇气。

He turned and asked in a low voice, "Can you lend me a thousand?"
他转过身，低声问道："你能借我一千块吗？"

"Sure," said O'Brien, dropping a heavy sack by the gold already.
"当然可以，"奥布莱恩说着，已经把一个沉重的袋子扔到了金子旁边。

"But truthfully, John, I don't believe the beast can do this."
"但说实话，约翰，我不相信那野兽能做到这一点。"

Everyone in the Eldorado Saloon rushed outside to see the event.
埃尔多拉多酒吧里的每个人都冲到外面观看这一幕。

They left tables and drinks, and even the games were paused.
他们离开了桌子和饮料，甚至游戏也暂停了。

Dealers and gamblers came to witness the bold wager's end.
庄家和赌徒们纷纷前来见证这场大胆赌注的结束。

Hundreds gathered around the sled in the icy open street.
数百人聚集在结冰的街道上的雪橇周围。

Matthewson's sled stood with a full load of flour sacks.
马修森的雪橇上满载着面粉袋。

The sled had been sitting for hours in minus temperatures.
雪橇已经在零度以下的气温中停放了几个小时。

The sled's runners were frozen tight to the packed-down snow.

雪橇的滑板被紧紧地冻在了厚厚的雪地上。

Men offered two-to-one odds that Buck could not move the sled.

人们以二比一的赔率赌巴克无法移动雪橇。

A dispute broke out about what "break out" really meant.

关于"突破"的真正含义，发生了争论。

O'Brien said Thornton should loosen the sled's frozen base.

奥布莱恩说，桑顿应该松开雪橇冻结的底座。

Buck could then "break out" from a solid, motionless start.

然后，巴克就可以从坚实、静止的状态下"突围"出来。

Matthewson argued the dog must break the runners free too.

马修森认为狗也必须把跑步者救出来。

The men who had heard the bet agreed with Matthewson's view.

听过赌注的人都同意马修森的观点。

With that ruling, the odds jumped to three-to-one against Buck.

根据这一裁决，巴克获胜的赔率上升到了三比一。

No one stepped forward to take the growing three-to-one odds.

没有人站出来承担越来越大的三比一赔率。

Not a single man believed Buck could perform the great feat.

没有一个人相信巴克能够完成这一伟大壮举。

Thornton had been rushed into the bet, heavy with doubts.

桑顿带着深深的疑虑匆忙参与了这场赌注。

Now he looked at the sled and the ten-dog team beside it.

现在他看着雪橇和旁边的十只狗组成的队伍。

Seeing the reality of the task made it seem more impossible.

看到这个任务的现实后，它看起来更加不可能了。

Matthewson was full of pride and confidence in that moment.

那一刻，马修森充满了自豪和自信。

"Three to one!" he shouted. "I'll bet another thousand, Thornton!
"三比一！"他喊道，"我再赌一千，桑顿！"

What do you say?" he added, loud enough for all to hear.
你说什么？"他补充道，声音大到所有人都能听到。

Thornton's face showed his doubts, but his spirit had risen.
桑顿脸上露出疑惑，但他的精神已经振奋起来。

That fighting spirit ignored odds and feared nothing at all.
那种战斗精神无视困难，无所畏惧。

He called Hans and Pete to bring all their cash to the table.
他叫来汉斯和皮特，让他们把所有的现金都拿到桌子上。

They had little left—only two hundred dollars combined.
他们所剩无几了——加起来只有两百美元。

This small sum was their total fortune during hard times.
这笔小钱就是他们艰难时期的全部财产。

Still, they laid all of the fortune down against Matthewson's bet.
尽管如此，他们还是把全部财产押在了马修森的赌注上。

The ten-dog team was unhitched and moved away from the sled.
十只狗组成的队伍被解开，离开了雪橇。

Buck was placed in the reins, wearing his familiar harness.
巴克被放在缰绳上，戴着他熟悉的挽具。

He had caught the energy of the crowd and felt the tension.
他感受到了人群的活力和紧张气氛。

Somehow, he knew he had to do something for John Thornton.
不管怎样，他知道他必须为约翰·桑顿做点什么。

People murmured with admiration at the dog's proud figure.
人们对这只狗骄傲的身影发出赞叹声。

He was lean and strong, without a single extra ounce of flesh.

他身材精瘦，体魄强健，身上没有一丝多余的肉。

His full weight of hundred fifty pounds was all power and endurance.

他的全部体重有一百五十磅，全靠力量和耐力。

Buck's coat gleamed like silk, thick with health and strength.

巴克的皮毛像丝绸一样闪闪发光，厚实而富有健康和力量。

The fur along his neck and shoulders seemed to lift and bristle.

他脖子和肩膀上的毛发似乎竖了起来。

His mane moved slightly, each hair alive with his great energy.

他的鬃毛微微摇曳，每一根毛发都散发着巨大的能量。

His broad chest and strong legs matched his heavy, tough frame.

他宽阔的胸膛和强壮的双腿与他厚重、坚韧的身材相得益彰。

Muscles rippled under his coat, tight and firm as bound iron.

他的外套下肌肉起伏，紧实如铁。

Men touched him and swore he was built like a steel machine.

人们触摸他并发誓他就像一台钢铁机器。

The odds dropped slightly to two to one against the great dog.

大狗获胜的几率略微下降为二比一。

A man from the Skookum Benches pushed forward, stuttering.

一名来自斯科库姆长凳的男子结结巴巴地向前走去。

"Good, sir! I offer eight hundred for him—before the test, sir!"

"好，先生！我出价八百英镑买下他——在考试之前，先生！"

"Eight hundred, as he stands right now!" the man insisted.
"就他现在的水平，八百！"那人坚持道。

Thornton stepped forward, smiled, and shook his head calmly.
桑顿走上前，微笑着，平静地摇了摇头。

Matthewson quickly stepped in with a warning voice and frown.
马修森皱着眉头，迅速走了进来，发出警告的声音。

"You must step away from him," he said. "Give him space."
"你必须离他远点，"他说，"给他点空间。"

The crowd grew silent; only gamblers still offered two to one.
人群安静下来，只有赌徒还在提供二比一的赌注。

Everyone admired Buck's build, but the load looked too great.
每个人都钦佩巴克的体格，但是负荷看起来太大了。

Twenty sacks of flour—each fifty pounds in weight—seemed far too much.
二十袋面粉——每袋重五十磅——似乎太多了。

No one was willing to open their pouch and risk their money.
没有人愿意打开自己的钱袋去冒险。

Thornton knelt beside Buck and took his head in both hands.
桑顿跪在巴克身边，双手捧着他的头。

He pressed his cheek against Buck's and spoke into his ear.
他把脸颊贴在巴克的脸颊上，对着他的耳朵说话。

There was no playful shaking or whispered loving insults now.
现在不再有嬉闹的摇晃或低声的爱意侮辱。

He only murmured softly, "As much as you love me, Buck."
他只是轻声低语道："就像你爱我一样，巴克。"

Buck let out a quiet whine, his eagerness barely restrained.
巴克发出一声安静的呜咽，几乎抑制不住他的渴望。

The onlookers watched with curiosity as tension filled the air.

旁观者好奇地看着气氛紧张。

The moment felt almost unreal, like something beyond reason.

那一刻感觉几乎不真实，就像某种超越理性的事情。

When Thornton stood, Buck gently took his hand in his jaws.

当桑顿站起来时，巴克轻轻地将他的手放在他的下巴上。

He pressed down with his teeth, then let go slowly and gently.

他用牙齿压下去，然后慢慢地、轻轻地放开。

It was a silent answer of love, not spoken, but understood.

这是爱的无声回答，没有说出口，但却心领神会。

Thornton stepped well back from the dog and gave the signal.

桑顿从狗身边退开一步，然后发出信号。

"Now, Buck," he said, and Buck responded with focused calm.

"现在，巴克，"他说道，巴克以专注而平静的态度回应。

Buck tightened the traces, then loosened them by a few inches.

巴克把牵引绳拉紧，然后又松开了几英寸。

This was the method he had learned; his way to break the sled.

这是他学到的方法；这是他打破雪橇的方法。

"Gee!" Thornton shouted, his voice sharp in the heavy silence.

"哎呀！"桑顿喊道，在寂静中他的声音很尖锐。

Buck turned to the right and lunged with all of his weight.

巴克向右转身，用尽全身的力气猛扑过去。

The slack vanished, and Buck's full mass hit the tight traces.

松弛消失了，巴克的整个身体都撞到了绷紧的绳索上
。

The sled trembled, and the runners made a crisp crackling sound.
雪橇颤动起来，滑行器发出清脆的噼啪声。

"Haw!" Thornton commanded, shifting Buck's direction again.
"哈！"桑顿命令道，再次改变了巴克的方向。

Buck repeated the move, this time pulling sharply to the left.
巴克重复了这一动作，这次他猛地向左拉。

The sled cracked louder, the runners snapping and shifting.
雪橇发出更响的噼啪声，滑板断裂并移动。

The heavy load slid slightly sideways across the frozen snow.
沉重的货物在冻雪上稍微向侧面滑动。

The sled had broken free from the grip of the icy trail!
雪橇已经脱离了冰道的束缚！

Men held their breath, unaware they were not even breathing.
人们屏住呼吸，没有意识到自己甚至没有呼吸。

"Now, PULL!" Thornton cried out across the frozen silence.
"现在，拉！"桑顿在一片寂静中大声喊道。

Thornton's command rang out sharp, like the crack of a whip.
桑顿的命令听起来很尖锐，就像鞭子抽打的声音。

Buck hurled himself forward with a fierce and jarring lunge.
巴克猛地向前猛冲，发出刺耳的撞击声。

His whole frame tensed and bunched for the massive strain.
由于承受着巨大的压力，他的整个身体都绷紧了。

Muscles rippled under his fur like serpents coming alive.
他的皮毛下的肌肉起伏不平，就像活过来的蛇一样。

His great chest was low, head stretched forward toward the sled.
他宽阔的胸膛低垂着，头向前伸向雪橇。

His paws moved like lightning, claws slicing the frozen ground.

他的爪子像闪电一样移动，爪子划过冰冻的地面。

Grooves were cut deep as he fought for every inch of traction.

他为了每一寸的牵引力而奋斗，留下了深深的伤痕。

The sled rocked, trembled, and began a slow, uneasy motion.

雪橇摇晃着，颤抖着，开始缓慢而不安地移动。

One foot slipped, and a man in the crowd groaned aloud.

一只脚滑了一下，人群中一名男子大声呻吟。

Then the sled lunged forward in a jerking, rough movement.

然后，雪橇猛地向前猛冲。

It didn't stop again—half an inch...an inch...two inches more.

它没有再停下来——

半英寸……一英寸……又两英寸。

The jerks became smaller as the sled began to gather speed.

随着雪橇速度的加快，颠簸变得越来越小。

Soon Buck was pulling with smooth, even, rolling power.

很快，巴克就能以平稳、均匀、滚动的力量拉动。

Men gasped and finally remembered to breathe again.

男人们倒吸一口气，终于想起来了。

They had not noticed their breath had stopped in awe.

他们没有注意到，自己的呼吸已经因敬畏而停止了。

Thornton ran behind, calling out short, cheerful commands.

桑顿跑在后面，大声喊着简短而欢快的命令。

Ahead was a stack of firewood that marked the distance.

前面有一堆柴火标记着距离。

As Buck neared the pile, the cheering grew louder and louder.

当巴克靠近那堆东西时，欢呼声越来越大。

The cheering swelled into a roar as Buck passed the end point.

当巴克越过终点时，欢呼声逐渐升华为咆哮声。

Men jumped and shouted, even Matthewson broke into a grin.

人们跳起来，欢呼起来，就连马修森也咧嘴笑了。

Hats flew into the air, mittens were tossed without thought or aim.

帽子在空中飞舞，手套被无意识地抛出。

Men grabbed each other and shook hands without knowing who.

男人们互相抓住对方并握手，却不知道是谁。

The whole crowd buzzed in wild, joyful celebration.

整个人群沸腾起来，欢欣雀跃。

Thornton dropped to his knees beside Buck with trembling hands.

桑顿双手颤抖地跪在巴克身边。

He pressed his head to Buck's and shook him gently back and forth.

他把巴克的头贴在巴克的头上，轻轻地前后摇晃。

Those who approached heard him curse the dog with quiet love.

走近的人听到他默默地咒骂那条狗。

He swore at Buck for a long time—softly, warmly, with emotion.

他大声咒骂巴克许久——

语气轻柔，热情洋溢，充满感情。

"Good, sir! Good, sir!" cried the Skookum Bench king in a rush.

"好的，先生！好的，先生！"斯科库姆长凳之王急忙喊道。

"I'll give you a thousand—no, twelve hundred—for that dog, sir!"

"先生，我愿意出一千——不，一千二百——
的价钱买这条狗！"

Thornton rose slowly to his feet, his eyes shining with emotion.

桑顿慢慢地站了起来，眼里闪烁着激动的光芒。

Tears streamed openly down his cheeks without any shame.
泪水毫无羞耻地顺着脸颊流下来。

"Sir," he said to the Skookum Bench king, steady and firm
"先生，"他坚定而坚定地对斯库库姆长凳之王说道

"No, sir. You can go to hell, sir. That's my final answer."
"不，先生。你下地狱吧，先生。这是我的最终答案。"

Buck grabbed Thornton's hand gently in his strong jaws.
巴克用强壮的下巴轻轻地抓住桑顿的手。

Thornton shook him playfully, their bond deep as ever.
桑顿开玩笑地摇了摇他，他们之间的感情依然深厚。

The crowd, moved by the moment, stepped back in silence.
人群被这一刻所感动，默默地后退。

From then on, none dared interrupt such sacred affection.
从此，再无人敢打扰如此神圣的感情。

The Sound of the Call
呼唤的声音

Buck had earned sixteen hundred dollars in five minutes.
巴克在五分钟内就赚了一千六百美元。

The money let John Thornton pay off some of his debts.
这笔钱让约翰·桑顿偿还了部分债务。

With the rest of the money he headed East with his partners.
他带着剩余的钱与合伙人一起前往东部。

They sought a fabled lost mine, as old as the country itself.
他们寻找一座传说中的失落矿井，其历史与这个国家一样悠久。

Many men had looked for the mine, but few had ever found it.
许多人都曾寻找过这座矿井，但很少有人找到它。

More than a few men had vanished during the dangerous quest.
在这次危险的探险中，有不少人失踪了。

This lost mine was wrapped in both mystery and old tragedy.
这座失落的矿井被神秘和古老的悲剧所笼罩。

No one knew who the first man to find the mine had been.
没有人知道第一个发现这座矿井的人是谁。

The oldest stories don't mention anyone by name.
最古老的故事没有提到任何人的名字。

There had always been an ancient ramshackle cabin there.
那里一直有一间古老而摇摇欲坠的小屋。

Dying men had sworn there was a mine next to that old cabin.
垂死之人发誓那间旧木屋旁边有一座矿井。

They proved their stories with gold like none found elsewhere.
他们用其他地方找不到的黄金证明了他们的故事。

No living soul had ever looted the treasure from that place.

从来没有人从那里掠夺过宝藏。

The dead were dead, and dead men tell no tales.
死者已死，死人不会留下任何痕迹。

So Thornton and his friends headed into the East.
于是桑顿和他的朋友们前往东部。

Pete and Hans joined, bringing Buck and six strong dogs.
皮特和汉斯也加入了进来，他们带来了巴克和六只强壮的狗。

They set off down an unknown trail where others had failed.
他们踏上了一条别人失败的未知道路。

They sledded seventy miles up the frozen Yukon River.
他们乘雪橇沿着冰冻的育空河逆流而上七十英里。

They turned left and followed the trail into the Stewart.
他们向左转，沿着小路进入斯图尔特。

They passed the Mayo and McQuestion, pressing farther on.
他们经过梅奥和麦奎森，继续前行。

The Stewart shrank into a stream, threading jagged peaks.
斯图尔特河逐渐变成一条小溪，穿过锯齿状的山峰。

These sharp peaks marked the very spine of the continent.
这些尖锐的山峰标志着这片大陆的脊梁。

John Thornton demanded little from men or the wild land.
约翰·桑顿对人类和荒野的要求很少。

He feared nothing in nature and faced the wild with ease.
他无所畏惧自然，能够轻松地面对荒野。

With only salt and a rifle, he could travel where he wished.
仅凭盐和一支步枪，他就能去任何他想去的地方。

Like the natives, he hunted food while he journeyed along.
像当地人一样，他在旅途中捕猎食物。

If he caught nothing, he kept going, trusting luck ahead.
如果他什么也没抓到，他就会继续前行，相信前方有好运。

On this long journey, meat was the main thing they ate.
在这次漫长的旅途中，肉是他们主要的食物。

The sled held tools and ammo, but no strict timetable.
雪橇上装有工具和弹药，但没有严格的时间表。

Buck loved this wandering; the endless hunt and fishing.
巴克喜欢这种漫游、无休止的狩猎和钓鱼。

For weeks they were traveling day after steady day.
连续数周，他们日复一日地奔波。

Other times they made camps and stayed still for weeks.
其他时候，他们会扎营并静静地待上数周。

The dogs rested while men dug through frozen dirt.
当人们在冻土中挖掘时，狗在休息。

They warmed pans over fires and searched for hidden gold.
他们将锅放在火上加热，寻找隐藏的黄金。

Some days they starved, and some days they had feasts.
有时候他们会挨饿，有时候他们会大吃大喝。

Their meals depended on the game and the luck of the hunt.
他们的食物取决于猎物和狩猎的运气。

When summer came, men and dogs packed loads on their backs.
夏天到来的时候，男人和狗就背起重物。

They rafted across blue lakes hidden in mountain forests.
他们乘木筏穿过隐藏在山林中的蓝色湖泊。

They sailed slim boats on rivers no man had ever mapped.
他们驾驶着细长的船，在从未有人绘制过地图的河流上航行。

Those boats were built from trees they sawed in the wild.
这些船是用他们在野外锯的树木建造的。

The months passed, and they twisted through the wild unknown lands.
几个月过去了，他们穿越了荒野的未知土地。

There were no men there, yet old traces hinted that men had been.
那里没有人类，但古老的痕迹却暗示着曾经有人存在。

If the Lost Cabin was real, then others had once come this way.

如果"迷失小屋"是真实存在的，那么其他人一定也曾来过这里。

They crossed high passes in blizzards, even during the summer.

即使是在夏天，他们也冒着暴风雪穿越山口。

They shivered under the midnight sun on bare mountain slopes.

他们在光秃秃的山坡上，在午夜的阳光下瑟瑟发抖。

Between the treeline and the snowfields, they climbed slowly.

他们在树线和雪原之间缓慢攀登。

In warm valleys, they swatted at clouds of gnats and flies.

在温暖的山谷中，他们拍打着成群的蚊虫和苍蝇。

They picked sweet berries near glaciers in full summer bloom.

他们在夏季盛开的冰川附近采摘甜浆果。

The flowers they found were as lovely as those in the Southland.

他们发现的花和南国的花一样美丽。

That fall they reached a lonely region filled with silent lakes.

那年秋天，他们到达了一个遍布寂静湖泊的荒凉地区。

The land was sad and empty, once alive with birds and beasts.

这片土地曾经充满鸟兽，如今却一片荒凉。

Now there was no life, just the wind and ice forming in pools.

现在没有生命，只有风和水池中形成的冰。

Waves lapped against empty shores with a soft, mournful sound.

海浪拍打着空旷的海岸，发出轻柔而悲伤的声音。

Another winter came, and they followed faint, old trails again.

又一个冬天来临，他们又沿着模糊的旧路前行。

These were the trails of men who had searched long before them.

这些是很久以前搜寻过的人们留下的足迹。

Once they found a path cut deep into the dark forest.

有一次，他们发现了一条深入黑暗森林的小路。

It was an old trail, and they felt the lost cabin was close.

这是一条古老的小路，他们感觉失踪的小屋就在附近。

But the trail led nowhere and faded into the thick woods.

但这条小路不知通向何方，消失在茂密的树林中。

Whoever made the trail, and why they made it, no one knew.

没人知道是谁开辟了这条小路，以及他们为何开辟这条小路。

Later, they found the wreck of a lodge hidden among the trees.

后来，他们在树林里发现了一间小屋的残骸。

Rotting blankets lay scattered where someone once had slept.

腐烂的毯子散落在曾经有人睡过的地方。

John Thornton found a long-barreled flintlock buried inside.

约翰·桑顿（John Thornton）
发现里面埋着一把长管燧发枪。

He knew this was a Hudson Bay gun from early trading days.

他从早期交易时就知道这是哈德逊湾枪。

In those days such guns were traded for stacks of beaver skins.

在那个年代，这种枪是用一堆海狸皮来交换的。

That was all—no clue remained of the man who built the lodge.

仅此而已——
没有留下任何关于建造这座小屋的人的线索。

Spring came again, and they found no sign of the Lost Cabin.
春天又来了，他们却没有发现迷失小屋的踪迹。

Instead they found a broad valley with a shallow stream.
他们发现的却是一片宽阔的山谷，山谷里有一条浅浅的小溪。

Gold lay across the pan bottoms like smooth, yellow butter.
金子铺满锅底，就像光滑的黄色黄油一样。

They stopped there and searched no farther for the cabin.
他们就在那里停了下来，不再寻找小屋。

Each day they worked and found thousands in gold dust.
他们每天辛勤劳作，在金粉中发现了数千颗金子。

They packed the gold in bags of moose-hide, fifty pounds each.
他们将黄金装入驼鹿皮袋中，每袋五十磅。

The bags were stacked like firewood outside their small lodge.
这些袋子像柴火一样堆放在他们的小屋外面。

They worked like giants, and the days passed like quick dreams.
他们像巨人一样努力工作，日子过得像做梦一样快。

They heaped up treasure as the endless days rolled swiftly by.
无数的日子一天天过去，他们积累了越来越多的财富。

There was little for the dogs to do except haul meat now and then.
除了偶尔运送肉以外，狗几乎没什么事可做。

Thornton hunted and killed the game, and Buck lay by the fire.
桑顿捕猎并杀死了猎物，而巴克则躺在火堆旁。

He spent long hours in silence, lost in thought and memory.
他长时间地保持沉默，沉浸在思考和回忆中。

The image of the hairy man came more often into Buck's mind.
那个毛茸茸的男人的形象越来越频繁地出现在巴克的脑海里。

Now that work was scarce, Buck dreamed while blinking at the fire.
现在工作很少了，巴克一边眨着眼睛看着火，一边做着梦。

In those dreams, Buck wandered with the man in another world.
在那些梦里，巴克和那个男人在另一个世界里流浪。

Fear seemed the strongest feeling in that distant world.
在那个遥远的世界里，恐惧似乎是最强烈的感觉。

Buck saw the hairy man sleep with his head bowed low.
巴克看到那个毛茸茸的男人低着头睡觉。

His hands were clasped, and his sleep was restless and broken.
他双手紧握，睡眠不安稳。

He used to wake with a start and stare fearfully into the dark.
他常常突然惊醒，并恐惧地盯着黑暗。

Then he'd toss more wood onto the fire to keep the flame bright.
然后他会把更多的木头扔进火里以保持火焰明亮。

Sometimes they walked along a beach by a gray, endless sea.
有时他们会沿着灰色、无边无际的海滩散步。

The hairy man picked shellfish and ate them as he walked.
毛人一边走，一边捡贝类吃。

His eyes searched always for hidden dangers in the shadows.
他的眼睛总是搜寻着阴影中隐藏的危险。

His legs were always ready to sprint at the first sign of threat.

一旦发现威胁，他的双腿就随时准备冲刺。

They crept through the forest, silent and wary, side by side.
他们并肩悄悄地、警惕地穿过森林。

Buck followed at his heels, and both of them stayed alert.
巴克紧随其后，两人都保持警惕。

Their ears twitched and moved, their noses sniffed the air.
他们的耳朵抽动着，鼻子嗅着空气。

The man could hear and smell the forest as sharply as Buck.
这个人能像巴克一样敏锐地听到并闻到森林的声音。

The hairy man swung through the trees with sudden speed.
毛茸茸的男人突然加速穿过树林。

He leapt from branch to branch, never missing his grip.
他从一个树枝跳到另一个树枝，始终抓不住树枝。

He moved as fast above the ground as he did upon it.
他在地面上移动的速度与他在地面上移动的速度一样快。

Buck remembered long nights beneath the trees, keeping watch.
巴克记得自己在树下守夜的漫长时光。

The man slept roosting in the branches, clinging tight.
男人睡在树枝上，紧紧地抱住树枝。

This vision of the hairy man was tied closely to the deep call.
毛人的这个景象与深沉的呼唤紧密相关。

The call still sounded through the forest with haunting force.
那呼唤声依然在森林中回荡，令人难以忘怀。

The call filled Buck with longing and a restless sense of joy.
这呼唤让巴克心中充满了渴望和一种不安的喜悦感。

He felt strange urges and stirrings that he could not name.
他感觉到一种难以名状的奇怪冲动和激动。

Sometimes he followed the call deep into the quiet woods.
有时他会追随呼唤，深入寂静的森林。

He searched for the calling, barking softly or sharply as he went.

他一边走一边寻找呼唤的声音，轻轻地或尖锐地吠叫。

He sniffed the moss and black soil where the grasses grew.

他嗅了嗅长满草的苔藓和黑土的味道。

He snorted with delight at the rich smells of the deep earth.

听到深层泥土的浓郁气味，他高兴地哼了一声。

He crouched for hours behind trunks covered in fungus.

他在长满真菌的树干后面蹲了几个小时。

He stayed still, listening wide-eyed to every tiny sound.

他一动不动，睁大眼睛聆听每一个细微的声音。

He may have hoped to surprise the thing that gave the call.

他或许希望给打电话的人一个惊喜。

He did not know why he acted this way—he simply did.

他不知道自己为何这么做——他只是这么做了。

The urges came from deep within, beyond thought or reason.

这种冲动源自内心深处，超越了思考或理性。

Irresistible urges took hold of Buck without warning or reason.

无法抗拒的冲动毫无预兆或理由地占据了巴克的心。

At times he was dozing lazily in camp under the midday heat.

有时，在正午的酷热中，他在营地里懒洋洋地打瞌睡。

Suddenly, his head lifted and his ears shoot up alert.

突然，他抬起头，警惕地竖起耳朵。

Then he sprang up and dash into the wild without pause.

然后他跳了起来，毫不停顿地冲进了荒野。

He ran for hours through forest paths and open spaces.

他在森林小径和空地上跑了几个小时。

He loved to follow dry creek beds and spy on birds in the trees.

他喜欢沿着干涸的河床行走并观察树上的鸟儿。

He could lie hidden all day, watching partridges strut around.

他可以整天躲藏着，看着鹧鸪四处走动。

They drummed and marched, unaware of Buck's still presence.

他们一边击鼓一边行进，完全没有注意到巴克还在。

But what he loved most was running at twilight in summer.

但他最喜欢的还是夏日黄昏时分的奔跑。

The dim light and sleepy forest sounds filled him with joy.

昏暗的灯光和令人昏昏欲睡的森林声音让他充满了喜悦。

He read the forest signs as clearly as a man reads a book.

他能像读书一样清楚地读出森林里的迹象。

And he searched always for the strange thing that called him.

他总是在寻找那召唤他的奇怪事物。

That calling never stopped — it reached him waking or sleeping.

那个呼唤从未停止——
无论他醒着还是睡着，它都能够听到。

One night, he woke with a start, eyes sharp and ears high.

一天夜里，他突然惊醒，眼睛锐利，耳朵竖起。

His nostrils twitched as his mane stood bristling in waves.

他的鼻孔抽动着，鬃毛竖起，像波浪一样。

From deep in the forest came the sound again, the old call.

森林深处再次传来声音，那古老的呼唤。

This time the sound rang clearly, a long, haunting, familiar howl.

这一次，声音很清晰，是一声悠长、萦绕心头、熟悉的嚎叫。

It was like a husky's cry, but strange and wild in tone.

它就像哈士奇的叫声，但语气奇怪而狂野。

Buck knew the sound at once—he had heard the exact sound long ago.

巴克立刻就听出了这个声音——

他很久以前就听过这个声音。

He leapt through camp and vanished swiftly into the woods.

他冲过营地，迅速消失在树林里。

As he neared the sound, he slowed and moved with care.

当他靠近声音时，他放慢了速度并小心翼翼地移动。

Soon he reached a clearing between thick pine trees.

很快他就到达了茂密松树之间的一片空地。

There, upright on its haunches, sat a tall, lean timber wolf.

那里，坐着一只高大、精瘦的森林狼。

The wolf's nose pointed skyward, still echoing the call.

狼的鼻子指向天空，仍然回荡着叫声。

Buck had made no sound, yet the wolf stopped and listened.

巴克没有发出任何声音，但狼却停下来听。

Sensing something, the wolf tensed, searching the darkness.

感觉到了什么，狼紧张起来，搜寻着黑暗。

Buck crept into view, body low, feet quiet on the ground.

巴克悄悄地出现在视野中，身体低垂，双脚静静地踩在地上。

His tail was straight, his body coiled tight with tension.

他的尾巴笔直，身体因紧张而紧紧蜷缩着。

He showed both threat and a kind of rough friendship.

他既表现出威胁，又表现出一种粗鲁的友谊。

It was the wary greeting shared by beasts of the wild.

这是野兽之间谨慎的问候。

But the wolf turned and fled as soon as it saw Buck.

但狼一看见巴克就转身逃跑了。

Buck gave chase, leaping wildly, eager to overtake it.

巴克疯狂地跳跃，追赶它，渴望追上它。

He followed the wolf into a dry creek blocked by a timber jam.

他跟着狼走进了一条被木材堵塞的干涸小溪。

Cornered, the wolf spun around and stood its ground.
狼被逼到绝境，转身站稳了脚跟。

The wolf snarled and snapped like a trapped husky dog in a fight.
狼像一只在战斗中被困住的哈士奇犬一样，发出咆哮和撕咬的声音。

The wolf's teeth clicked fast, its body bristling with wild fury.
狼的牙齿快速咬合，身上充满狂野的怒火。

Buck did not attack but circled the wolf with careful friendliness.
巴克没有发起攻击，而是小心翼翼地友好地绕着狼转圈。

He tried to block his escape by slow, harmless movements.
他试图通过缓慢、无害的动作来阻止自己逃跑。

The wolf was wary and scared—Buck outweighed him three times.
狼很警惕，也很害怕——巴克的体重是它的三倍。

The wolf's head barely reached up to Buck's massive shoulder.
狼的头刚好够到巴克宽阔的肩膀。

Watching for a gap, the wolf bolted and the chase began again.
狼发现空隙后，拔腿就跑，追逐再次开始。

Several times Buck cornered him, and the dance repeated.
巴克多次将他逼到角落，然后又重复同样的舞蹈。

The wolf was thin and weak, or Buck could not have caught him.
这只狼又瘦又弱，否则巴克不可能抓住它。

Each time Buck drew near, the wolf spun and faced him in fear.
每当巴克靠近时，狼就会转身并惊恐地面对他。

Then at the first chance, he dashed off into the woods once more.
然后，他一有机会，就再次冲进了树林。

But Buck did not give up, and finally the wolf came to trust him.

但巴克没有放弃，最终狼终于信任了他。

He sniffed Buck's nose, and the two grew playful and alert.

他嗅了嗅巴克的鼻子，两只巴克变得嬉戏又警觉起来。

They played like wild animals, fierce yet shy in their joy.

他们像野生动物一样玩耍，快乐时凶猛，但又害羞。

After a while, the wolf trotted off with calm purpose.

过了一会儿，狼平静地小跑着走开了。

He clearly showed Buck that he meant to be followed.

他清楚地向巴克表示他想要被跟踪。

They ran side by side through the twilight gloom.

他们并肩奔跑在暮色中。

They followed the creek bed up into the rocky gorge.

他们沿着河床走进岩石峡谷。

They crossed a cold divide where the stream had begun.

他们穿过了溪流起源处的寒冷分水岭。

On the far slope they found wide forest and many streams.

在远处的山坡上，他们发现了广阔的森林和许多溪流。

Through this vast land, they ran for hours without stopping.

在这片广袤的土地上，他们不停地奔跑了几个小时。

The sun rose higher, the air grew warm, but they ran on.

太阳越来越高，天气越来越暖，但他们仍继续奔跑。

Buck was filled with joy—he knew he was answering his calling.

巴克心里充满了喜悦——
他知道他正在回应他的召唤。

He ran beside his forest brother, closer to the call's source.

他跑到森林兄弟身边，靠近呼唤声的来源。

Old feelings returned, powerful and hard to ignore.

旧日的感情又回来了，强烈而难以忽视。

These were the truths behind the memories from his dreams.

这就是他梦中记忆的真相。

He had done all this before in a distant and shadowy world.

他曾经在一个遥远而阴暗的世界里做过这一切。

Now he did this again, running wild with the open sky above.

现在他又这样做了，在开阔的天空下狂奔。

They stopped at a stream to drink from the cold flowing water.

他们在一条小溪边停下来喝冰凉的流水。

As he drank, Buck suddenly remembered John Thornton.

喝酒的时候，巴克突然想起了约翰·桑顿。

He sat down in silence, torn by the pull of loyalty and the calling.

他默默地坐了下来，忠诚和使命的牵引让他心力交瘁。

The wolf trotted on, but came back to urge Buck forward.

狼继续小跑，但又回来催促巴克前进。

He sniffed his nose and tried to coax him with soft gestures.

他嗅了嗅他的鼻子，并试图用温柔的动作哄他。

But Buck turned around and started back the way he came.

但巴克却转身，沿着来时的路返回。

The wolf ran beside him for a long time, whining quietly.

狼在他旁边跑了很久，小声地哀嚎着。

Then he sat down, raised his nose, and let out a long howl.

然后他坐下来，抬起鼻子，发出一声长长的嚎叫。

It was a mournful cry, softening as Buck walked away.

这是一声悲伤的哭喊，随着巴克走开，哭喊声渐渐减弱了。

Buck listened as the sound of the cry faded slowly into the forest silence.

巴克听着哭喊声渐渐消失在森林的寂静中。

John Thornton was eating dinner when Buck burst into the camp.

当巴克冲进营地时，约翰·桑顿正在吃晚饭。

Buck leapt upon him wildly, licking, biting, and tumbling him.

巴克疯狂地向他扑来，舔他、咬他、把他推倒。

He knocked him over, scrambled on top, and kissed his face.

他把他打倒，爬到他身上，亲吻他的脸。

Thornton called this "playing the general tom-fool" with affection.

桑顿深情地将此称为"愚弄大众"。

All the while, he cursed Buck gently and shook him back and forth.

他一直轻轻地咒骂着巴克，并来回摇晃他。

For two whole days and nights, Buck never left the camp once.

整整两天两夜，巴克一次也没有离开营地。

He kept close to Thornton and never let him out of his sight.

他一直跟在桑顿身边，从不让他离开自己的视线。

He followed him as he worked and watched him while he ate.

他跟着他干活，看着他吃饭。

He saw Thornton into his blankets at night and out each morning.

他看到桑顿每天晚上钻进毯子里，早上又钻出毯子。

But soon the forest call returned, louder than ever before.

但很快森林的呼唤又回来了，而且比以前更加响亮。

Buck grew restless again, stirred by thoughts of the wild wolf.

巴克又开始焦躁起来，他一想到野狼就烦躁不安。

He remembered the open land and running side by side.

他记得在开阔的土地上并肩奔跑。

He began wandering into the forest once more, alone and alert.

他再次独自一人，警惕地走进森林。

But the wild brother did not return, and the howl was not heard.

可是野性兄弟没有回来，也没有听到嚎叫。

Buck started sleeping outside, staying away for days at a time.

巴克开始在外面睡觉，一次出去好几天。

Once he crossed the high divide where the creek had begun.

有一次，他越过了小溪源头处的高分水岭。

He entered the land of dark timber and wide flowing streams.

他进入了一片有着深色木材和宽阔溪流的土地。

For a week he roamed, searching for signs of the wild brother.

他四处游荡了一周，寻找野生兄弟的踪迹。

He killed his own meat and travelled with long, tireless strides.

他亲手宰杀了肉，然后迈着不知疲倦的长步前进。

He fished for salmon in a wide river that reached the sea.

他在一条流入大海的宽阔河流中捕捞鲑鱼。

There, he fought and killed a black bear maddened by bugs.

在那里，他与一只被虫子逼疯的黑熊搏斗并杀死了它。

The bear had been fishing and ran blindly through the trees.

这只熊一直在钓鱼，然后盲目地在树林里奔跑。

The battle was a fierce one, waking Buck's deep fighting spirit up.

战斗十分激烈，唤醒了巴克深厚的战斗精神。

Two days later, Buck returned to find wolverines at his kill.

两天后，巴克回来发现狼獾正围着他的猎物。

A dozen of them quarreled over the meat in noisy fury.

他们十几个人为了肉吵吵闹闹、争吵不休。

Buck charged and scattered them like leaves in the wind.

巴克冲了过来，把他们像风中的落叶一样吹散了。

Two wolves remained behind—silent, lifeless, and unmoving forever.

留下了两只狼——沉默、毫无生气、永远一动不动。

The thirst for blood grew stronger than ever.

对鲜血的渴望比以往任何时候都更加强烈。

Buck was a hunter, a killer, feeding off living creatures.
巴克是一名猎人、一名杀手，以活物为食。

He survived alone, relying on his strength and sharp senses.
他依靠自己的力量和敏锐的感觉独自生存了下来。

He thrived in the wild, where only the toughest could live.
他在野外茁壮成长，那里只有最坚强的人才能生存。

From this, a great pride rose up and filled Buck's whole being.
从此，一股巨大的自豪感油然而生，充满了巴克的整个身心。

His pride showed in his every step, in the ripple of every muscle.
他的每一个脚步、每一块肌肉的波动都彰显着他的骄傲。

His pride was as clear as speech, seen in how he carried himself.
他的骄傲就像言语一样明显，从他的举止中可以看出来。

Even his thick coat looked more majestic and gleamed brighter.
就连他厚厚的皮毛也显得更加威严、更加闪亮。

Buck could have been mistaken for a giant timber wolf.
巴克可能会被误认为是一只巨大的森林狼。

Except for brown on his muzzle and spots above his eyes.
除了口鼻部是棕色的，眼睛上方有斑点。

And the white streak of fur that ran down the middle of his chest.
还有一条白色的毛发从他的胸部中央垂下来。

He was even larger than the biggest wolf of that fierce breed.
他甚至比那种凶猛品种中最大的狼还要大。

His father, a St. Bernard, gave him size and heavy frame.
他的父亲是一只圣伯纳犬，赋予了他高大魁梧的体格。

His mother, a shepherd, shaped that bulk into wolf-like form.
他的母亲是一位牧羊人，她将这个庞然大物塑造成了狼的形状。

He had the long muzzle of a wolf, though heavier and broader.
他有着像狼一样的长嘴，但更重、更宽。

His head was a wolf's, but built on a massive, majestic scale.
他的头是狼头，但体型巨大，威严雄伟。

Buck's cunning was the cunning of the wolf and of the wild.
巴克的狡猾是狼的狡猾，是野性的狡猾。

His intelligence came from both the German Shepherd and St. Bernard.
他的智力既来自德国牧羊犬，也来自圣伯纳犬。

All this, plus harsh experience, made him a fearsome creature.
所有这些，再加上严酷的经历，使他成为一个可怕的生物。

He was as formidable as any beast that roamed the northern wild.
他和北方荒野中游荡的任何野兽一样强大。

Living only on meat, Buck reached the full peak of his strength.
巴克只吃肉，体力就达到了顶峰。

He overflowed with power and male force in every fiber of him.
他的每一个细胞都充满着力量和男性的力量。

When Thornton stroked his back, the hairs sparked with energy.
当桑顿抚摸他的背部时，他的毛发便闪烁着活力。

Each hair crackled, charged with the touch of living magnetism.
每根头发都发出噼啪声，充满了活生生的磁力。

His body and brain were tuned to the finest possible pitch.
他的身体和大脑已经调整到了最佳状态。

Every nerve, fiber, and muscle worked in perfect harmony.
每根神经、纤维和肌肉都完美地协调运作。

To any sound or sight needing action, he responded instantly.
对于任何需要采取行动的声音或景象，他都会立即做出反应。

If a husky leaped to attack, Buck could leap twice as fast.
如果哈士奇跳起来攻击，巴克可以跳得快两倍。

He reacted quicker than others could even see or hear.
他的反应比其他人看到或听到的还要快。

Perception, decision, and action all came in one fluid moment.
感知、决策和行动都在一个流畅的时刻发生。

In truth, these acts were separate, but too fast to notice.
事实上，这些行为是分开的，但速度太快而难以察觉。

So brief were the gaps between these acts, they seemed as one.
这些动作之间的间隔非常短暂，看起来就像一个动作。

His muscles and being was like tightly coiled springs.
他的肌肉和身躯就像紧紧盘绕的弹簧一样。

His body surged with life, wild and joyful in its power.
他的身体充满了生命力，充满狂野和快乐。

At times he felt like the force was going to burst out of him entirely.
有时他感觉力量就要从他体内完全爆发出来。

"Never was there such a dog," Thornton said one quiet day.
"从来没有过这样的狗，" 桑顿在一个平静的日子里说道。

The partners watched Buck striding proudly from the camp.
伙伴们看着巴克骄傲地大步走出营地。

"When he was made, he changed what a dog can be," said Pete.

皮特说："当他被创造出来时，他改变了狗的本质。"

"By Jesus! I think so myself," Hans quickly agreed.
"天哪！我自己也这么认为，"汉斯很快就同意了。

They saw him march off, but not the change that came after.
他们看见他离开，却没有看到随后发生的变化。

As soon as he entered the woods, Buck transformed completely.
一进入树林，巴克就完全变了样。

He no longer marched, but moved like a wild ghost among trees.
他不再行进，而是像树林中的野鬼一样移动。

He became silent, cat-footed, a flicker passing through shadows.
他变得沉默不语，脚步轻快，身影在阴影中闪动。

He used cover with skill, crawling on his belly like a snake.
他熟练地利用掩护，像蛇一样匍匐前进。

And like a snake, he could leap forward and strike in silence.
就像一条蛇，他可以悄无声息地向前跳跃并发起攻击。

He could steal a ptarmigan straight from its hidden nest.
他可以直接从隐藏的巢穴中偷走一只雷鸟。

He killed sleeping rabbits without a single sound.
他悄无声息地杀死了熟睡的兔子。

He could catch chipmunks midair as they fled too slowly.
他可以在半空中抓住逃跑速度太慢的花栗鼠。

Even fish in pools could not escape his sudden strikes.
就连池塘里的鱼也无法逃脱他的突然袭击。

Not even clever beavers fixing dams were safe from him.
甚至连修缮水坝的聪明海狸也无法逃脱他的攻击。

He killed for food, not for fun—but liked his own kills best.
他杀生是为了食物，而不是为了乐趣——
但他最喜欢自己杀死的猎物。

Still, a sly humor ran through some of his silent hunts.
尽管如此，他的一些无声狩猎中仍流露出一种狡黠的幽默。

He crept up close to squirrels, only to let them escape.
他悄悄靠近松鼠，却让它们逃走了。

They were going to flee to the trees, chattering in fearful outrage.
它们正要逃到树林里，一边发出恐惧和愤怒的声音。

As fall came, moose began to appear in greater numbers.
随着秋天的到来，驼鹿的数量开始增多。

They moved slowly into the low valleys to meet the winter.
它们慢慢地迁入低谷，度过冬天。

Buck had already brought down one young, stray calf.
巴克已经捕获了一头迷路的小牛犊。

But he longed to face larger, more dangerous prey.
但他渴望面对更大、更危险的猎物。

One day on the divide, at the creek's head, he found his chance.
有一天，在分水岭上，在小溪的源头，他找到了机会。

A herd of twenty moose had crossed from forested lands.
一群二十头驼鹿从森林地带走过来。

Among them was a mighty bull; the leader of the group.
其中有一头威武的公牛，它是这群公牛的首领。

The bull stood over six feet tall and looked fierce and wild.
这头公牛身高超过六英尺，看上去凶猛而狂野。

He tossed his wide antlers, fourteen points branching outward.
他摇晃着宽大的鹿角，十四个角向外分叉。

The tips of those antlers stretched seven feet across.
这些鹿角的尖端长达七英尺。

His small eyes burned with rage as he spotted Buck nearby.
当他发现巴克在附近时，他的小眼睛里燃起了愤怒的火焰。

He let out a furious roar, trembling with fury and pain.

他发出一声愤怒的咆哮，因愤怒和痛苦而颤抖。

An arrow-end stuck out near his flank, feathered and sharp.

一支箭尖从他的侧腹附近伸出，呈羽毛状，十分锋利。

This wound helped explain his savage, bitter mood.

这处伤口解释了他野蛮、痛苦的情绪。

Buck, guided by ancient hunting instinct, made his move.

巴克在古老的狩猎本能的指引下采取了行动。

He aimed to separate the bull from the rest of the herd.

他的目的是将这头公牛与其他牛群区分开。

This was no easy task—it took speed and fierce cunning.

这不是一件容易的事——它需要速度和敏锐的智慧。

He barked and danced near the bull, just out of range.

他在公牛附近吠叫并跳舞，但刚好超出了它的射程。

The moose lunged with huge hooves and deadly antlers.

驼鹿用巨大的蹄子和致命的鹿角猛扑过来。

One blow could have ended Buck's life in a heartbeat.

一次打击就可能瞬间结束巴克的生命。

Unable to leave the threat behind, the bull grew mad.

公牛无法摆脱威胁，变得疯狂。

He charged in fury, but Buck always slipped away.

他愤怒地冲锋，但巴克总是溜走。

Buck faked weakness, luring him farther from the herd.

巴克假装虚弱，引诱他远离牛群。

But young bulls were going to charge back to protect the leader.

但年轻的公牛会冲回来保护领头牛。

They forced Buck to retreat and the bull to rejoin the group.

他们迫使巴克撤退，并迫使公牛重新加入群体。

There is a patience in the wild, deep and unstoppable.

野性中蕴藏着一种忍耐，深沉而不可阻挡。

A spider waits motionless in its web for countless hours.

一只蜘蛛在网中一动不动地等待了无数个小时。

A snake coils without twitching, and waits till it is time.
蛇盘绕着身体，不抽搐，等待时机成熟。

A panther lies in ambush, until the moment arrives.
一只豹子埋伏着，等待时机到来。

This is the patience of predators who hunt to survive.
这是为了生存而狩猎的掠食者的耐心。

That same patience burned inside Buck as he stayed close.
当巴克靠近他时，他的心里也燃烧着同样的耐心。

He stayed near the herd, slowing its march and stirring fear.
他待在牛群附近，减缓牛群的行进速度并引起恐惧。

He teased the young bulls and harassed the mother cows.
他戏弄小公牛并骚扰母牛。

He drove the wounded bull into a deeper, helpless rage.
他让受伤的公牛陷入更深的、无助的狂怒之中。

For half a day, the fight dragged on with no rest at all.
足足有半天的时间，战斗一直持续着，没有丝毫的停歇。

Buck attacked from every angle, fast and fierce as wind.
巴克从各个角度发起攻击，速度快如风，凶猛如风。

He kept the bull from resting or hiding with its herd.
他阻止公牛休息或与牛群一起躲藏。

Buck wore down the moose's will faster than its body.
巴克消灭驼鹿的意志比消灭它的身体的速度还快。

The day passed and the sun sank low in the northwest sky.
一天过去了，太阳低低地沉入西北的天空。

The young bulls returned more slowly to help their leader.
年轻的公牛慢慢地返回去帮助它们的首领。

Fall nights had returned, and darkness now lasted six hours.
秋夜又回来了，黑暗持续了六个小时。

Winter was pressing them downhill into safer, warmer valleys.
冬天迫使他们下山，进入更安全、更温暖的山谷。

But still they couldn't escape the hunter that held them back.
但他们仍然无法逃脱阻止他们的猎人。

Only one life was at stake—not the herd's, just their leader's.

只有一个人的生命受到威胁——

不是牛群的生命，而是牛群首领的生命。

That made the threat distant and not their urgent concern.

这使得威胁变得遥远，不再是他们迫切需要关注的问题。

In time, they accepted this cost and let Buck take the old bull.

最终，他们接受了这个代价并让巴克带走了这头老公牛。

As twilight settled in, the old bull stood with his head down.

暮色降临，老公牛低着头站着。

He watched the herd he had led vanish into the fading light.

他看着自己带领的牛群消失在渐渐暗淡的光线中。

There were cows he had known, calves he had once fathered.

那里有他认识的母牛，也有他曾经养育过的小牛。

There were younger bulls he had fought and ruled in past seasons.

在过去的几个季节里，他曾与一些年轻的公牛搏斗并获胜。

He could not follow them—for before him crouched Buck again.

他无法跟随他们——因为巴克又蹲在他面前。

The merciless fanged terror blocked every path he might take.

这只长着无情尖牙的恐怖怪物挡住了他的每一条路。

The bull weighed more than three hundredweight of dense power.

这头公牛体重超过三百磅，蕴含着强大的力量。

He had lived long and fought hard in a world of struggle.

他活了很久，并在充满斗争的世界中努力奋斗。

Yet now, at the end, death came from a beast far beneath him.

然而现在，最终，死亡却来自远在他之下的野兽。

Buck's head did not even rise to the bull's huge knuckled knees.

巴克的头甚至没有抬到公牛巨大的膝盖。

From that moment on, Buck stayed with the bull night and day.

从那一刻起，巴克就日夜和公牛呆在一起。

He never gave him rest, never allowed him to graze or drink.

他从不让他休息，从不让他吃草或喝水。

The bull tried to eat young birch shoots and willow leaves.

公牛试图吃嫩桦树芽和柳树叶。

But Buck drove him off, always alert and always attacking.

但巴克把他赶走了，他始终保持警惕，不断发起攻击。

Even at trickling streams, Buck blocked every thirsty attempt.

即使在涓涓细流旁，巴克也会阻止每一次口渴的尝试。

Sometimes, in desperation, the bull fled at full speed.

有时，公牛绝望了，会全速逃跑。

Buck let him run, loping calmly just behind, never far away.

巴克让他跑，自己则在后面平静地奔跑，不远离。

When the moose paused, Buck lay down, but stayed ready.

当驼鹿停下来时，巴克躺下，但仍保持准备状态。

If the bull tried to eat or drink, Buck struck with full fury.

如果公牛试图吃东西或喝水，巴克就会愤怒地攻击它。

The bull's great head sagged lower under its vast antlers.

公牛的大脑袋在巨大的鹿角下低垂着。

His pace slowed, the trot became a heavy; a stumbling walk.

他的步伐慢了下来，小跑变得沉重，步履蹒跚。

He often stood still with drooped ears and nose to the ground.

他经常静静地站着，耳朵和鼻子耷拉在地上。

During those moments, Buck took time to drink and rest.
在那些时刻，巴克会花时间喝水和休息。

Tongue out, eyes fixed, Buck sensed the land was changing.
巴克伸出舌头，双眼凝视，感觉到土地正在发生变化。

He felt something new moving through the forest and sky.
他感觉到森林和天空中有一些新的东西在移动。

As moose returned, so did other creatures of the wild.
随着驼鹿的回归，其他野生动物也随之回归。

The land felt alive with presence, unseen but strongly known.
这片土地充满生机，虽然看不见，却又为人熟知。

It was not by sound, sight, nor by scent that Buck knew this.
巴克并不是通过声音、视觉或嗅觉知道这一点的。

A deeper sense told him that new forces were on the move.
一种更深层次的感觉告诉他，新的力量正在行动。

Strange life stirred through the woods and along the streams.
奇异的生命在树林和溪流间活跃起来。

He resolved to explore this spirit, after the hunt was complete.
狩猎结束后，他决定探索这个灵魂。

On the fourth day, Buck brought down the moose at last.
第四天，巴克终于把驼鹿打倒了。

He stayed by the kill for a full day and night, feeding and resting.
他在猎物旁边呆了一整天一夜，进食、休息。

He ate, then slept, then ate again, until he was strong and full.
他吃饭、睡觉，然后再吃饭，直到他强壮、饱足。

When he was ready, he turned back toward camp and Thornton.
当他准备好时，他转身返回营地和桑顿。

With steady pace, he began the long return journey home.
他迈着稳健的步伐，开始了漫长的归途。

He ran in his tireless lope, hour after hour, never once straying.

他不知疲倦地奔跑，一个小时又一个小时，从未走失。

Through unknown lands, he moved straight as a compass needle.

在穿越未知的土地时，他像指南针一样笔直地前进。

His sense of direction made man and map seem weak by comparison.

相比之下，他的方向感让人类和地图都显得无力。

As Buck ran, he felt more strongly the stir in the wild land.

巴克越跑，就越强烈地感受到荒野的骚动。

It was a new kind of life, unlike that of the calm summer months.

这是一种新的生活，不同于平静的夏季生活。

This feeling no longer came as a subtle or distant message.

这种感觉不再是一种微妙或遥远的信息。

Now the birds spoke of this life, and squirrels chattered about it.

现在鸟儿们谈论着这种生活，松鼠们也喋喋不休地谈论着它。

Even the breeze whispered warnings through the silent trees.

甚至连微风在寂静的树林间低声发出警告。

Several times he stopped and sniffed the fresh morning air.

他多次停下来，呼吸着早晨的新鲜空气。

He read a message there that made him leap forward faster.

他在那里读了一条信息，这让他向前跳跃得更快了。

A heavy sense of danger filled him, as if something had gone wrong.

一种浓重的危机感弥漫在他的心头，仿佛有什么事情出了差错。

He feared calamity was coming—or had already come.

他担心灾难即将来临——或者已经来临。

He crossed the last ridge and entered the valley below.

他越过最后一座山脊，进入了下面的山谷。

He moved more slowly, alert and cautious with every step.
他走得更慢了，每一步都警惕而谨慎。

Three miles out he found a fresh trail that made him stiffen.
走出三英里后，他发现了一条新鲜的小路，这让他感到一阵僵硬。

The hair along his neck rippled and bristled in alarm.
他脖子上的毛发惊恐地竖了起来。

The trail led straight toward the camp where Thornton waited.
这条小路笔直通向桑顿等候的营地。

Buck moved faster now, his stride both silent and swift.
巴克现在走得更快了，他的步伐既安静又迅速。

His nerves tightened as he read signs others were going to miss.
当他看到别人可能忽略的迹象时，他的神经变得紧张起来。

Each detail in the trail told a story—except the final piece.
小径上的每一个细节都讲述着一个故事——
除了最后一段。

His nose told him about the life that had passed this way.
他的鼻子告诉他这条路上过去的生活。

The scent gave him a changing picture as he followed close behind.
当他紧随其后时，气味使他看到了不断变化的画面。

But the forest itself had gone quiet; unnaturally still.
但森林本身却变得安静，异常安静。

Birds had vanished, squirrels were hidden, silent and still.
鸟儿消失了，松鼠也躲了起来，静静地。

He saw only one gray squirrel, flat on a dead tree.
他只看到一只灰松鼠趴在一棵枯树上。

The squirrel blended in, stiff and motionless like a part of the forest.

松鼠融入其中，僵硬而一动不动，就像森林的一部分。

Buck moved like a shadow, silent and sure through the trees.
巴克像影子一样移动，悄无声息、坚定地穿过树林。

His nose jerked sideways as if pulled by an unseen hand.
他的鼻子猛地向一侧歪去，仿佛被一只看不见的手拉扯着。

He turned and followed the new scent deep into a thicket.
他转身，循着新的气味走进了灌木丛深处。

There he found Nig, lying dead, pierced through by an arrow.
他发现尼格躺在那里死了，身上被箭射穿。

The shaft passed clear through his body, feathers still showing.
箭杆穿透了他的身体，羽毛仍然露出。

Nig had dragged himself there, but died before reaching help.
尼格拖着自己到达那里，但在得到救援之前就死了。

A hundred yards farther on, Buck found another sled dog.
再往前走一百码，巴克发现了另一只雪橇犬。

It was a dog that Thornton had bought back in Dawson City.
这是桑顿在道森市买回来的一只狗。

The dog was in a death struggle, thrashing hard on the trail.
这只狗正在进行殊死挣扎，在路上拼命挣扎。

Buck passed around him, not stopping, eyes fixed ahead.
巴克从他身边走过，没有停留，眼睛直视前方。

From the direction of the camp came a distant, rhythmic chant.
从营地方向传来一阵遥远而有节奏的吟唱声。

Voices rose and fell in a strange, eerie, sing-song tone.
声音以一种奇怪、怪异、唱歌般的音调响起又落下。

Buck crawled forward to the edge of the clearing in silence.
巴克默默地爬到空地的边缘。

There he saw Hans lying face-down, pierced with many arrows.

他看到汉斯面朝下躺着，身上中了许多箭。

His body looked like a porcupine, bristling with feathered shafts.

他的身体看上去像一只豪猪，身上长满了羽毛。

At the same moment, Buck looked toward the ruined lodge.

与此同时，巴克看向了那间被毁坏的小屋。

The sight made the hair rise stiff on his neck and shoulders.

这一幕让他脖子和肩膀上的汗毛都竖了起来。

A storm of wild rage swept through Buck's whole body.

狂暴的怒火席卷了巴克的全身。

He growled aloud, though he did not know that he had.

他大声咆哮，尽管他不知道自己已经咆哮了。

The sound was raw, filled with terrifying, savage fury.

那声音很生硬，充满了恐怖、野蛮的愤怒。

For the last time in his life, Buck lost reason to emotion.

巴克一生中最后一次失去了理智，被情感所笼罩。

It was love for John Thornton that broke his careful control.

正是对约翰·桑顿的爱打破了他小心翼翼的控制。

The Yeehats were dancing around the wrecked spruce lodge.

伊哈特人正在被毁坏的云杉小屋周围跳舞。

Then came a roar—and an unknown beast charged toward them.

随后传来一声咆哮——
一只不知名的野兽向他们冲来。

It was Buck; a fury in motion; a living storm of vengeance.

那是巴克；是一股正在运动的狂怒；是一场活生生的复仇风暴。

He flung himself into their midst, mad with the need to kill.

他冲进他们中间，疯狂地想要杀戮。

He leapt at the first man, the Yeehat chief, and struck true.

他向第一个人，也就是 Yeehat 酋长，猛扑过去，击中了他。

His throat was ripped open, and blood spouted in a stream.
他的喉咙被撕开，鲜血喷涌而出。

Buck did not stop, but tore the next man's throat with one leap.
巴克没有停下来，而是一跃而起，撕开了下一个人的喉咙。

He was unstoppable—ripping, slashing, never pausing to rest.
他势不可挡——不断撕扯、砍杀，永不停歇。

He darted and sprang so fast their arrows could not touch him.
他飞快地冲刺，以至于他们的箭无法射到他。

The Yeehats were caught in their own panic and confusion.
耶哈特人也陷入了自己的恐慌和困惑之中。

Their arrows missed Buck and struck one another instead.
他们的箭没有射中巴克，而是射中了彼此。

One youth threw a spear at Buck and hit another man.
一名年轻人向巴克扔了一支长矛，并击中了另一个人。

The spear drove through his chest, the point punching out his back.
长矛刺穿了他的胸膛，矛尖刺穿了他的后背。

Terror swept over the Yeehats, and they broke into full retreat.
恐惧席卷了耶哈特人，他们全线撤退。

They screamed of the Evil Spirit and fled into the forest shadows.
他们尖叫着害怕恶魔并逃进了森林的阴影中。

Truly, Buck was like a demon as he chased the Yeehats down.
确实，当巴克追击耶哈特人时，他就像一个恶魔。

He tore after them through the forest, bringing them down like deer.
他穿过森林追赶他们，像猎杀鹿一样将他们击倒。

It became a day of fate and terror for the frightened Yeehats.

对于惊恐万分的耶哈特人来说，这一天成为了命运和恐怖的一天。

They scattered across the land, fleeing far in every direction.
他们四散逃窜，逃往各地。

A full week passed before the last survivors met in a valley.
整整一周后，最后的幸存者在山谷中相遇。

Only then did they count their losses and speak of what happened.
直到那时，他们才计算自己的损失并讲述所发生的事情。

Buck, after tiring of the chase, returned to the ruined camp.
巴克追逐累了之后，返回了被毁坏的营地。

He found Pete, still in his blankets, killed in the first attack.
他发现皮特还盖着毯子，在第一次袭击中丧生。

Signs of Thornton's last struggle were marked in the dirt nearby.
附近的泥土上留下了桑顿最后一次挣扎的痕迹。

Buck followed every trace, sniffing each mark to a final point.
巴克跟踪着每一条踪迹，嗅探着每一个痕迹，直到找到最终的点。

At the edge of a deep pool, he found faithful Skeet, lying still.
在一个深水池边，他发现忠实的斯基特一动不动地躺着。

Skeet's head and front paws were in the water, unmoving in death.
斯基特的头和前爪浸在水中，一动不动，一命呜呼。

The pool was muddy and tainted with runoff from the sluice boxes.
水池很泥泞，被水闸箱里的径流污染了。

Its cloudy surface hid what lay beneath, but Buck knew the truth.

阴云密布的表面掩盖了其下的东西，但巴克知道真相
。

He tracked Thornton's scent into the pool—but the scent led nowhere else.
他循着桑顿的气味来到水池里——
但是这气味却没有指向别处。

There was no scent leading out—only the silence of deep water.
没有散发出任何气味——只有深水的寂静。

All day Buck stayed near the pool, pacing the camp in grief.
巴克整天待在水池附近，悲伤地在营地里踱步。

He wandered restlessly or sat in stillness, lost in heavy thought.
他或焦躁不安地徘徊，或静静地坐着，陷入沉思。

He knew death; the ending of life; the vanishing of all motion.
他知道死亡；生命的终结；一切运动的消失。

He understood that John Thornton was gone, never to return.
他知道约翰·桑顿已经走了，永远不会回来了。

The loss left an empty space in him that throbbed like hunger.
失去让他心里空落落的，像饥饿一样悸动。

But this was a hunger food could not ease, no matter how much he ate.
但这是一种食物无法缓解的饥饿，无论他吃多少。

At times, as he looked at the dead Yeehats, the pain faded.
有时，当他看到死去的伊哈特人时，痛苦就消失了。

And then a strange pride rose inside him, fierce and complete.
然后，他内心深处升起一股奇怪的骄傲，强烈而彻底
。

He had killed man, the highest and most dangerous game of all.
他杀死了人类，这是最高级、最危险的游戏。

He had killed in defiance of the ancient law of club and fang.

他违反了棍棒和尖牙的古老法则而杀人。

Buck sniffed their lifeless bodies, curious and thoughtful.

巴克好奇而又若有所思地嗅着它们毫无生气的身体。

They had died so easily—much easier than a husky in a fight.

他们死得太容易了——比打架的哈士奇死得还容易。

Without their weapons, they had no true strength or threat.

没有武器，他们就没有真正的力量或威胁。

Buck was never going to fear them again, unless they were armed.

巴克再也不会害怕他们了，除非他们带着武器。

Only when they carried clubs, spears, or arrows he'd beware.

只有当他们携带棍棒、长矛或箭时他才会小心。

Night fell, and a full moon rose high above the tops of the trees.

夜幕降临，一轮圆月高高地升起在树梢之上。

The moon's pale light bathed the land in a soft, ghostly glow like day.

月亮的苍白光芒笼罩着大地，使大地笼罩在柔和、幽灵般的光芒之中，如同白昼。

As the night deepened, Buck still mourned by the silent pool.

夜色越来越深，巴克依然在寂静的水池边哀悼。

Then he became aware of a different stirring in the forest.

然后他意识到森林里有不一样的动静。

The stirring was not from the Yeehats, but from something older and deeper.

这种激动并非来自耶哈特人，而是来自某种更古老、更深层次的东西。

He stood up, ears lifted, nose testing the breeze with care.

他站起来，竖起耳朵，用鼻子仔细地感受着微风。

From far away came a faint, sharp yelp that pierced the silence.

远处传来一声微弱而尖锐的尖叫，划破了寂静。

Then a chorus of similar cries followed close behind the first.

紧接着，又是一阵类似的哭喊声。

The sound drew nearer, growing louder with each passing moment.

声音越来越近，而且越来越大。

Buck knew this cry—it came from that other world in his memory.

巴克熟悉这声叫喊——

它来自他记忆中的另一个世界。

He walked to the center of the open space and listened closely.

他走到空地中央，仔细聆听。

The call rang out, many-noted and more powerful than ever.

号召响起，引起了广泛关注，并且比以往任何时候都更加强大。

And now, more than ever before, Buck was ready to answer his calling.

现在，巴克比以往任何时候都更愿意响应他的召唤。

John Thornton was dead, and no tie to man remained within him.

约翰·桑顿已经死了，他与人类的联系已不复存在。

Man and all human claims were gone—he was free at last.

人类和所有人类的权利都消失了——他终于自由了。

The wolf pack were chasing meat like the Yeehats once had.

狼群像耶哈特人曾经做的那样追逐肉食。

They had followed moose down from the timbered lands.

他们跟着驼鹿从林地下来。

Now, wild and hungry for prey, they crossed into his valley.

现在，它们变得狂野，渴望猎物，于是进入了他的山谷。

Into the moonlit clearing they came, flowing like silver water.

他们来到月光下的空地上，像银色的水一样流淌。

Buck stood still in the center, motionless and waiting for them.

巴克静静地站在中心，一动不动地等待着他们。

His calm, large presence stunned the pack into a brief silence.

他平静而高大的身影让狼群陷入短暂的沉默。

Then the boldest wolf leapt straight at him without hesitation.

然后，最大胆的狼毫不犹豫地直接向他扑来。

Buck struck fast and broke the wolf's neck in a single blow.

巴克迅速出击，一击就折断了狼的脖子。

He stood motionless again as the dying wolf twisted behind him.

当垂死的狼在他身后扭动时，他再次一动不动地站着。

Three more wolves attacked quickly, one after the other.

又有三只狼迅速发动了攻击，一只接一只。

Each retreated bleeding, their throats or shoulders slashed.

他们每个人都流着血撤退，喉咙或肩膀被割破。

That was enough to trigger the whole pack into a wild charge.

这足以引发整个狼群的疯狂冲锋。

They rushed in together, too eager and crowded to strike well.

他们一起冲了进来，因为太急切和拥挤而无法进行有效打击。

Buck's speed and skill allowed him to stay ahead of the attack.

巴克的速度和技巧使他在进攻中保持领先。

He spun on his hind legs, snapping and striking in all directions.

他用后腿旋转，向各个方向猛击和攻击。

To the wolves, this seemed like his defense never opened or faltered.

对于狼队来说，这看起来就像他的防守从未打开或动摇过。

He turned and slashed so quickly they could not get behind him.

他转身猛砍，速度之快让他们根本无法追上他。

Nonetheless, their numbers forced him to give ground and fall back.

尽管如此，敌军人数众多，迫使他退却。

He moved past the pool and down into the rocky creek bed.

他穿过水池，来到岩石河床。

There he came up against a steep bank of gravel and dirt.

在那里，他遇到了一处陡峭的砾石和泥土堤岸。

He edged into a corner cut during the miners' old digging.

他挤进了矿工们以前挖掘时挖出的一个角落。

Now, protected on three sides, Buck faced only the front wolf.

现在，巴克受到了三面保护，只需面对最前面的狼。

There, he stood at bay, ready for the next wave of assault.

他在那里坚守阵地，准备迎接下一波攻击。

Buck held his ground so fiercely that the wolves drew back.

巴克死命坚守阵地，狼群都向后退缩了。

After half an hour, they were worn out and visibly defeated.

半小时后，他们已经筋疲力尽，明显失败了。

Their tongues hung out, their white fangs gleamed in moonlight.

它们的舌头伸出来，白色的尖牙在月光下闪闪发光。

Some wolves lay down, heads raised, ears pricked toward Buck.

一些狼躺下，抬起头，竖起耳朵看着巴克。

Others stood still, alert and watching his every move.

其他人则站着不动，警惕地注视着他的一举一动。

A few wandered to the pool and lapped up cold water.

一些人漫步到水池边，舔着冷水。

Then one long, lean gray wolf crept forward in a gentle way.

然后，一只瘦长的灰狼温和地爬了过来。

Buck recognized him—it was the wild brother from before.

巴克认出了他——他就是之前的那个野蛮兄弟。

The gray wolf whined softly, and Buck replied with a whine.

灰狼轻轻地哀嚎了一声，巴克也用哀嚎回应。

They touched noses, quietly and without threat or fear.

他们轻轻地碰了碰鼻子，没有任何威胁或恐惧。

Next came an older wolf, gaunt and scarred from many battles.

接下来是一只年长的狼，它因多次战斗而憔悴不堪，身上满是伤疤。

Buck started to snarl, but paused and sniffed the old wolf's nose.

巴克开始咆哮，但停下来嗅了嗅老狼的鼻子。

The old one sat down, raised his nose, and howled at the moon.

老的那只坐下来，扬起鼻子，对着月亮嚎叫。

The rest of the pack sat down and joined in the long howl.

其余的狼也坐下来，加入长嚎。

And now the call came to Buck, unmistakable and strong.

现在，巴克收到了一个明确而强烈的呼唤。

He sat down, lifted his head, and howled with the others.

他坐下来，抬起头，和其他人一起嚎叫。

When the howling ended, Buck stepped out of his rocky shelter.

当嚎叫声结束时，巴克走出了岩石庇护所。

The pack closed in around him, sniffing both kindly and warily.

狼群围住了他，既友善又警惕地嗅着他的气息。

Then the leaders gave the yelp and dashed off into the forest.

然后领头的那群狼大叫一声，冲进了森林。

The other wolves followed, yelping in chorus, wild and fast in the night.

其他狼也紧随其后，齐声嚎叫，在夜色中狂野而迅速。

Buck ran with them, beside his wild brother, howling as he ran.

巴克和他们一起奔跑，在他那野性的兄弟旁边，一边跑一边嚎叫。

Here, the story of Buck does well to come to its end.

到这里，巴克的故事终于结束了。

In the years that followed, the Yeehats noticed strange wolves.

在随后的几年里，伊哈特人注意到了奇怪的狼。

Some had brown on their heads and muzzles, white on the chest.

有些动物的头部和口鼻部呈棕色，胸部呈白色。

But even more, they feared a ghostly figure among the wolves.

但他们更害怕狼群中出现的幽灵。

They spoke in whispers of the Ghost Dog, leader of the pack.

他们低声谈论着这群狗的首领——幽灵狗。

This Ghost Dog had more cunning than the boldest Yeehat hunter.

这只幽灵狗比最大胆的 Yeehat 猎人还要狡猾。

The ghost dog stole from camps in deep winter and tore their traps apart.

幽灵狗在隆冬时节从营地偷走东西并撕碎了陷阱。

The ghost dog killed their dogs and escaped their arrows without a trace.

鬼狗杀死了他们的狗，躲过了他们的箭，无影无踪。

Even their bravest warriors feared to face this wild spirit.

即使是最勇敢的战士也害怕面对这个野蛮的灵魂。

No, the tale grows darker still, as the years pass in the wild.

不，随着荒野中岁月的流逝，故事变得更加黑暗。

Some hunters vanish and never return to their distant camps.

一些猎人消失了，再也没有回到遥远的营地。

Others are found with their throats torn open, slain in the snow.

其他人被发现喉咙被撕开，被杀害在雪地里。

Around their bodies are tracks—larger than any wolf could make.

它们的身体周围有足迹——
比任何狼留下的足迹都要大。

Each autumn, Yeehats follow the trail of the moose.

每年秋天，耶哈特人都会追寻驼鹿的踪迹。

But they avoid one valley with fear carved deep into their hearts.

但他们避开了一个山谷，因为恐惧深深地刻在了他们的心里。

They say the valley is chosen by the Evil Spirit for his home.

据说这个山谷是恶魔选定的家园。

And when the tale is told, some women weep beside the fire.

当这个故事被讲述出来时，一些妇女在火堆旁哭泣。

But in summer, one visitor comes to that quiet, sacred valley.

但到了夏天，一位游客来到了那座安静、神圣的山谷。

The Yeehats do not know of him, nor could they understand.

耶哈特人不认识他，也无法理解他。

The wolf is a great one, coated in glory, like no other of his kind.

这只狼非常伟大，浑身散发着荣耀，与同类中其他狼都不一样。

He alone crosses from green timber and enters the forest glade.

他独自一人穿过绿色树林，进入森林空地。

There, golden dust from moose-hide sacks seeps into the soil.

在那里，驼鹿皮袋里的金色粉末渗入土壤。

Grass and old leaves have hidden the yellow from the sun.

草和老叶遮住了阳光下的黄色。

Here, the wolf stands in silence, thinking and remembering.

在这里，狼默默地站着，思考着，回忆着。

He howls once—long and mournful—before he turns to go.

他转身离开之前，发出一声漫长而悲伤的嚎叫。

Yet he is not always alone in the land of cold and snow.

然而，在这片寒冷冰雪的土地上，他并不总是孤独的。

When long winter nights descend on the lower valleys.

当漫长的冬夜降临低洼山谷时。

When the wolves follow game through moonlight and frost.

当狼群在月光和霜冻中追逐猎物时。

Then he runs at the head of the pack, leaping high and wild.

然后他跑在队伍的最前面，高高跃起，狂野不已。

His shape towers over the others, his throat alive with song.

他的身形高大，嗓音中充满歌声。

It is the song of the younger world, the voice of the pack.

这是年轻世界的歌声，是狼群的声音。

He sings as he runs—strong, free, and forever wild.

他一边奔跑一边歌唱——坚强、自由、永远狂野。